T0372544

Welcome Problems, Find Success

Creating Toyota Cultures Around the World

Kiyoshi "Nate" Furuta

Foreword by John Shook

Lean Global Network

Routledge
Taylor & Francis Group

First Published 2022
by Routledge
6000 Broken Sound Parkway #300, Boca Raton FL, 33487

and by Routledge
2 Park Square, Milton Park, Abingdon, Oxon, OX14 4RN

Routledge is an imprint of the Taylor & Francis Group, an informa business

Library of Congress Cataloging-in-Publication Data
A catalog record for this title has been requested

ISBN: 978-1-032-06593-9 (hbk)
ISBN: 978-1-032-06592-2 (pbk)
ISBN: 978-1-003-20296-7 (ebk)

Contents

Foreword
by John Shook

"Furuta-san is a monster." That's what my boss at Toyota said to me after a meeting with Nate Furuta in late 1983. We had been in a planning meeting during the earliest stages of what would later become known as NUMMI (New United Motor Manufacturing Inc.), the company's joint venture with General Motors. Nate was in charge of key pieces, such as the Toyota way of working, human resources, and labor relations.

In subsequent years, the Toyota Production System (TPS), then lean thinking, and then the Toyota Way would become famous. Over the ensuing decades, most pieces of the system would become well understood by many, even as the means by which to apply the pieces in diverse, real-world settings would remain elusive to most.

Culture is often tossed up as a catch-all concept for everything in an organization that can't be quantified or easily explained in mechanical terms. But using a compelling term, such as "culture," doesn't solve anything unless we can break it down into concrete, actionable terms. To build a strong organizational culture, nothing is more central than the pieces Nate oversaw at NUMMI: the Toyota way of working, human resources, and labor relations (NUMMI was a union shop).

Human resource management (HRM), including labor relations, is often considered a pain-in-the-ass afterthought, a job for people who can't do anything more important, or a mysterious black box of unnecessary complex and arcane policies and procedures. Not so in Toyota's system.

In the pages to come, Nate will take you along as he and others lead Toyota's intense globalization, from the early 1980s to recent days. He will introduce you to famous characters, like Taiichi Ohno and Fujio Cho, and lesser-known executives, like Kenzo Tamai, the head of the company's HRM function in the 1980s. Explaining the central role of HRM, Mr. Tamai told me,

> Human Resources is so important, we can say 'no' even to the president. Our policies and thinking are fundamental to the company's culture, so they shouldn't be altered easily based simply on any one person's opinion or wish of the moment. It takes five years to truly understand the effect of a change in basic HR policy. If our values, such as respecting the humanity of each employee, are held sincerely, we need to be conservative about changing policies until we learn their impact. But don't misunderstand: HR is not the point. We aren't here to be a good at HR; we are here to sell better cars to more people.

To me and many others to follow, this was an example of the kind of Toyota thinking that flew in the face of conventional wisdom and, like holding two opposing thoughts together at once, characterized the deep thinking that lay underneath every decision of the company: to find success, welcome your problems.

This is not a book about HRM policies and procedures. This is a deep dive into the way senior leaders embody deep awareness of HRM matters, developing and executing company strategy while at the same time developing human capability. The role of senior leaders isn't just a matter of directing the company to achieve objectives; it is a matter of building the capability to achieve those objectives, consistently, and further developing capability as it executes.

Key to this is to develop the awareness, attitude, capability, and practice of identifying problems as progress toward achieving objectives, which is, in fact, attained through steadfastly attacking each problem as it arises. This becomes a self-reinforcing loop of the organization, tapping in to the essence of solving problems while simultaneously developing ever better problem-solving skills and better problem solvers. This loop propels an organization toward meeting its purpose while developing capability for capability development.

This is no minor attainment or aspiration. It requires a "revolution in consciousness," as Ohno put it, and nowhere is the revolution greater than in managers' attitudes toward problems. Every manager wants success. Does every manager welcome problems? Nate argues that, if managers can learn to welcome problems, they can find paths forward to building organizations capable of the greatest success.

At the meeting that inspired my boss to call Nate a monster, Nate had been, well, not a monster, but forceful—winning arguments by the strength of his knowledge, combined with passion and coupled with vision and a sense of deep responsibility. What my boss meant by "monster"—he used a Japanized English term in the middle of a Japanese conversation and context—was that Nate had powerfully presented a way forward that would not be easy but would lead to success if we faced the uncertain road ahead with a clear vision, held our values sincerely, and adjusted to the twists and turns with open minds, welcoming the problems to come as the ultimate means of learning our way to success.

In the following pages, Nate will share—for the first time in print—his bold actions and points of view that informed Toyota's phenomenal success in creating Toyota cultures around the world, beginning with a crazy three-way venture (with General Motors and the UAW) in California, to a wholly-owned, non-union operation in Kentucky, to the complex environment that is the European automobile industry. (*Note*: There is no actual

"European automobile industry"—the challenges began right there.) Then finally back to the US for some mending, rework, and key innovations.

You will find no road map in these pages. You will find some guideposts and a great many deep insights to aid you in developing your own organizational culture, inspired, if you wish, by Toyota's efforts during the company's period of great globalization. Good luck in welcoming the problems that aren't just in the way, but can lead the way to your organization's greatest successes.

John Shook
Senior Advisor, Lean Enterprise Institute
Chairman, Lean Global Network

Introduction

Many executives have chased the Toyota model of success. You may be one whose organization has tried to replicate the Toyota Production System (TPS) and methods, such as *just-in-time* or *jidoka*. You probably found it difficult to achieve success, or when you did make improvements, to sustain success.

This book *will not* show you how to emulate TPS. But it will help you understand the *thinking* that inspired Toyota executives and work forces for decades. The basic thinking is simple: executives cannot solve a problem if they cannot find the problem. Just like a mistake-proofing system on a plant floor that surfaces problems, executives need tools and methods to surface problems. Because your problems are likely large and complex, you need to connect the specific problems you find with underlying causes of problems throughout your organization. To do that, you need to inspire everyone in your organization to find problems.

Toyota became successful because its executives were determined to create a culture dedicated to finding *Toyota's problems* then aligning solutions to those problems with *Toyota's vision*. TPS is the culmination of many of those solutions. You and your organization must learn to find *your problems* and develop solutions that align with *your vision*. Toyota's tools and techniques may be part of that solution, or they may not, and that depends on the problems you find.

"No problem, no kaizen" has become a catchphrase to promote problem solving, yet the casualness with which it is thrown about belies its importance. In fact, how Toyota lives that phrase—with relentless problem-finding and problem-solving attitude aligned with a shared vision—is the key to Toyota's basic thinking and success.

Many organizations have failed to sustain success because they never realized their problems or they uncovered their key problems too late to remain competitive.

Bringing attention to problems sometimes seems to go against human nature. Too often people prefer to ignore, hide, or work around problems, and in many cultures pointing out your own problems brings shame and disgrace. To instill a problem-finding mind set in which you and your employees are dedicated to surfacing and highlighting problems, you need to change culture, and to change culture you need to change behaviors. At Toyota it was necessary to change behaviors for problem finding and problem solving to flourish. And it required a pragmatic, grounded approach—there was no magic. Toyota's problem-finding, *kaizen* culture was systematically developed and it took decades to articulate to people outside of Toyota. It took great effort to make it stick even within Toyota.

Welcome Problems, Find Success: Building Toyota Cultures Around the World will describe the kaizen culture within Toyota that drove its success, and the relentless search for problems that emanated from that culture. You will learn about systems and techniques they successfully used to find significant problems, and to develop and sustain kaizen cultures at new global operations as they were developing. This book will help you to:

1. Establish systems that promote problem finding and problem solving from the top (you!) down.

2. Break complex corporate problems into more graspable, addressable smaller problems.

3. Create problems (!) for your organization in order to maintain a continuous problem-finding culture.

4. Embed systems that take problem finding from conscious decisions to personal habit.

Finding problems is too often considered a means only to address production issues—defects, delays, inefficiency, injuries. It does do that. But Toyota's problem-finding philosophies and kaizen culture are even more important for senior leadership. They help executives locate problems that can slowly build, multiply, and destroy an organization. This book is for corporate management—senior executives, vice presidents, directors, plant managers—and for any function within a company, from accounting to R&D. As a manager, you are key to your company adopting a problem-finding mind set and a kaizen culture.

During my 37 years with Toyota and three years with Toyoda Boshoku, I was presented unique management challenges. With every challenge, I had to identify problems that could prevent Toyota from achieving its vision. I had to establish problem-finding philosophies and build kaizen culture in new environments for Toyota—North America and Europe.

There is a good reason why Toyota sent me, a human-resources executive, to spearhead overseas ventures. Toyota had never assigned an HR executive to such a role, but the company recognized that success in new lands would rely on leadership and team members willing to find problems in these new locations. We did not expect this to come naturally. We needed to change people's behaviors.

There is a misperception that everyone at Toyota "gets it," that we walked into our roles, frontline assembly worker or vice president, and were automatically assimilated into the Toyota culture and able to grasp Toyota philosophies, concepts, tools, and techniques. Nothing could be further from the truth. Everyone within Toyota had to work to develop and sustain a problem-finding/kaizen mind, and it was management's role to make that happen and provide the coaching, mentoring, motivation, and systems to further that development.

For example, I joined Toyota in 1970 after graduating from the University of Tokyo with a bachelor of law degree, but I was in no way destined to work for Toyota nor equipped with a kaizen mind. I was assigned to Human Resources. Two executives there helped to shape my problem finding and problem solving abilities: Kenzo Tamai and Iwao Isomura. I worked for both within Toyota Human Resources as I developed proposals to address union demands and resolve grievances at our Japan plants. This work took me to every imaginable area of Toyota, forcing me to understand processes as if I were working the line (union perspective) or managing team members (company perspective).

Mr. Tamai taught me to analyze data and phenomena in order to clearly identify a problem, to accurately see facts, and to build countermeasures from those facts. My proposals to Mr. Tamai were repeatedly returned, crossed in red ink: I had not collected enough facts from the workplace to support my solution to a problem, to properly identify root causes, or to even define the problem correctly.

Mr. Tamai's network kept him in regular communications with the workforce—he knew ten thousand individuals by name— and he often knew the facts far better than those working under him could hope to discover. Based on information from his many contacts, he could have told me what was wrong with my proposal, but he did not. With repeated failures, I would check the facts again and again, returning to the workplace, listening to people, observing the physical conditions—even late at night to see the second shift.

Mr. Tamai was very logical and pragmatic, in order to ensure that a proposal would be accepted by the union and related departments. He encouraged me to be likewise: "Furuta, your fact finding is weak, your root cause analysis is insufficient, and your execution plan is not well thought through. Think deeper and come back with a better idea."

One day, I was really struggling with how to solve a union demand. Mr. Tamai told me to try and see the data from an entirely different perspective, which opened my eyes to the actual problem and led to a proposal that the union accepted. Over time I fought through his red ink and finally developed a successful proposal. As evidence of Mr. Tamai's approval, late one night after the union agreed to our proposal, I found a bottle of Johnnie Walker in my desk drawer.

In 1985, Mr. Tamai, as the head of HRM in Toyota, gave me full discretion to negotiate the all-important labor contract for NUMMI (Toyota-General Motors joint venture, New United Motor Manufacturing) with the UAW in North America without headquarters approval: a humbling vote of confidence from teacher to student.

My other teacher, Mr. Isomura, taught me to take a bird's eye view of problems. He was famous for taking the most complicated issue, quickly finding its substance, and ensuring that solutions clearly addressed the original problem. The speed with which Mr. Isomura worked and his big-picture perspective fit my nature.

While working with him I resolved a union demand in Japan to establish a 10 billion yen family-welfare fund for Toyota employees. Toyota considered the demand impossible because of the impact from taxes on funding and the interest, but by examining all possibilities of Japanese tax exemptions (bird's eye view) and analyzing every fact conceivable (carefully reviewing existing pension fund regulations), I negotiated with the Japan Treasury and the Ministry of Welfare to establish the Toyota family-welfare fund without any taxation. This fund is the only one of its kind in Japan because the government changed its interpretation of the law immediately after Toyota established the fund. (I once heard that Mr. Isomura regarded me as one of the top three individuals in Toyota he wanted for difficult tasks. He passed away before I could ask him who the other two were.)

The mentoring of Mr. Tamai and Mr. Isomura provided me with two contrasting but complimentary problem-finding skills, both of which served me well as I sought out and tackled the massive problems at Toyota:

- Leading labor negotiations in the early-1980s with the UAW to establish the Toyota-General Motors joint venture NUMMI in Fremont, California.

- Starting Toyota's first greenfield plant in North America in the late-1980s in Georgetown, Kentucky.

- Organizing corporate Toyota to better address globalization by establishing Toyota Motor North America manufacturing headquarters in Erlanger, Kentucky in the 1990s.

- Leading management to support Toyota DNA to reinvigorate manufacturing organizations, including sagging Georgetown at the turn of the century.

- Reviving Toyota's failing European division in the early 2000s .

Each of these roles presented myriad challenges for Toyota, and it was my job to find the problems behind these challenges and to clarify and resolve them. How I did that—and enlisted those around me to find and solve problems that aligned with Toyota's vision—helped me to better understand kaizen culture and what is needed to build a company of problem finders.

1. No Problem, No Improvement

NUMMI

Large organizations evolve organically over decades. Often, the resulting organization is an amalgam of good and bad practices cobbled together into systems that drive management and employee behaviors to unintended consequences. By contrast, Toyota executives, during its half century of incredible success, focused intentionally on managing the company's evolution, establishing systems that demand and encourage problem-finding behaviors, and spur improvements toward a shared, aligned vision. Such a problem-finding, improvement-minded culture (kaizen culture) depends upon individuals changing the way they think and act.

In 1982, in response to localization pressure from the US government, Toyota looked to establish a joint venture in California, particularly in a union environment, to see if Toyota practices could translate overseas. After a potential deal with Ford failed to materialize, I was told to head to the United States and meet with General Motors and the UAW to establish a legal framework to accommodate Toyota's kaizen culture in a UAW facility. My role was to develop a Letter of Intent (LOI) as the preliminary understanding of labor relations in the pending NUMMI joint venture and to draft the labor contract with the UAW once the joint venture was established.

I was surprised to be selected. I was a legal department assistant manager who had only transferred from Labor Relations a year earlier, did not speak English, and had no knowledge of the United States. I knew Japanese law and labor union practices because I had spent 12 years in Labor Relations, but I would need to intimately understand US labor law and UAW practices. I was appointed along with Mamoru (Mike) Furuhashi, an assistant manager in Human Resources who spoke fluent English.

The GM plant in Fremont, CA had been closed after 22 years of operation. Its workforce had filed more than 4,000 grievances, and absenteeism was over 20 percent. Due to a UAW demand, General Motors requested Toyota to staff production from the Fremont union ranks. In return, Toyota demanded that the UAW agree to a framework in Toyota and UAW documents that would allow workers to find and solve problems and continuously improve operations, which would be key to NUMMI succeeding.

It is a fundamental belief of Toyota that management and the workforce must relentlessly eliminate nonvalue-creating work, processes, jobs, functions, and projects, and redeploy extra resources to value-creating activities. This means that as an organization pursues a shared vision and evolves, instead of the traditional adversarial relationship, its members and their work practices are flexible and evolve as well. The UAW would need to agree to flexible work practices. Flexible work practices are a fundamental element of Toyota culture and its ability to find problems, experiment with changes to address them, implement changes, and improve.

The contract between GM and Toyota was signed Feb. 17, 1983 by Roger Smith and Eiji Toyoda. It had a contingency clause to establish a harmonious relationship with the UAW to enact the contract. We selected former US Secretary of Labor William Usery Jr. to be the negotiator with UAW President Owen Bieber, as a way for us to gain a basic understanding of labor relations. We provided Usery with TPS concepts, as well as the minimum requirements we would ask of the UAW. We successfully obtained these requirements, including introduction of TPS with flexible work practices, in the LOI dated Sept. 22, 1983. This allowed the company to establish the initial terms and conditions of employment and pledged a harmonious relationship between parties to negotiate the final contract by the end of June 1985.

Flexible work practices—such as a minimum number job classification, flexible production standards, kaizen program, company-initiated transfer of employees between work assignments, no lockouts, a no-strike clause with binding arbitration, limited seniority, broader mandatory overtime—were agreed to by the UAW in the LOI. But there was no guarantee they could be incorporated in a final contract. In fact, AAI—the Mazda-Ford joint venture under negotiation at the same time—failed to obtain a flexible work practices agreement in the labor contract for the Flat Rock, MI, facility. This happened even though it had secured the identical Letter of Intent from the UAW soon after our preliminary negotiations with the UAW.

Early in our negotiations, the union shop committee, which had not been part of the LOI negotiations but represented the majority in the final contract negotiation, presented to NUMMI management the old GM contract clauses as their proposal. The UAW local was, essentially, proposing that we run the plant like the GM plant that had been shuttered. I reminded the UAW of the contingency clause and that we would revoke the joint venture if we could not agree on a harmonious relationship. In other words, no flexible work practices and TPS, no NUMMI.

I had heard that UAW President Walter Ruther had told members that the role of the union was to establish and defend "production standards" to protect workers from the abuse of management. This was a cornerstone of the UAW's mission.

Production standards would certainly kill TPS, because TPS constantly requires finding and resolving problems, pursuing better processes, and eliminating waste. It was my personal responsibility to negotiate the work practices—including this contentious issue of "production standards"—because no American within NUMMI management understood Toyota's work practices to the level that I did. Because the production standard was so important to the UAW, Dick Shoemaker, assistant to UAW President Bieber, negotiated with me one on one.

This issue was critical to the UAW and Toyota. But we had a huge gap in understanding that this was the critical problem that needed to solve. Toyota utilized standardized work charts to define pace and process—not "production standards," as defined traditionally in the US auto industry. The standardized work charts described the step-by-step production process for each worker, the time required for each step, the amount of work-in-process inventory to hold, as well as many safety and quality points to be checked. The operator must follow this standard procedure, but anyone—often the operator—can change it if they find a better or easier way, with the approval of the immediate line supervisor or group leader. This was very dissimilar to the traditional US production standard.

The initial setup of standardized work is done by a team leader, who also is a union member, and not by industrial engineers (i.e., management). Given this condition, the pace of the operation is reasonable and sustainable from an operator's perspective, but future improvement is expected. The key distinction is that a union member, in this case the team leader, designs the initial work process under the assumption that the operator knows best his/her own operation.

Well, the Toyota approach and my initial descriptions simply frustrated my UAW counterpart. He could not imagine how to actualize our flexible practices. I spent countless hours in conversation with Shoemaker—working many late nights, sometimes arguing and sometimes talking over a few beers as we tried to understand one another. I described how flexible practices would work within Fremont and with a UAW workforce.

Eventually, we agreed to use their terminology, but our definition. When I described standardized work as a "production standard," Shoemaker had familiar terminology he could take back to Bieber. Shoemaker eventually bought in that it was the initiative of workers to set up the so-called production standard—

not management—and accepted our description of production standards (standardized but flexible work practices).

I believe that incorporating flexible work practices into the contract was the essential concession we got from the UAW and, most importantly, laid out the mutual trust concept for the UAW and NUMMI. Resolving this problem enabled Toyota to establish operations at NUMMI with a workforce authorized to find and solve problems and make improvements.

Toyota was able to plant the seed of kaizen culture in Fremont. On Dec. 10, 1984, eight months after the Federal Trade Commission approved NUMMI, Toyota, GM, and proud UAW workers launched the Fremont-built Nova with the highest quality rating in GM history. Flexible work practices remained in place until the end of the joint venture in 2010.

What is Your Problem?

What is your problem? This simple question is the key to finding a problem—and solving it. Everyone, starting with the CEO, must find problems that prevent an organization from reaching a shared vision. If there is no problem, there is no continuous improvement (kaizen). Having worked all over the globe, I've seen how leaders and managers everywhere struggle to find their place in a problem-finding culture and why it is so difficult to ask, "What is your problem?" Senior leadership should hold a spotlight to dramatically illuminate problems. However, we often see them:

- View problems in a negative light (as do those who assess their performance) and see association with problems as worse than other employees because they are supposed to have everything under control. ("No problem.")

- Think they should delegate problem finding and problem solving because their job is to deal only with big issues.

- Don't know how to find problems and don't know their role in problem finding.

- Afraid they won't know how to solve a problem when they find one.

- Unwilling to admit their own mistakes, to highlight their own problems.

By contrast, Toyota leaders and managers ask, *What is your problem?*—of others and themselves—thousands of times a year. In doing so, they create an environment where kaizen is pursued relentlessly and, more importantly, one in which managers nurture a problem-finding culture in the organization. Toyota managers have been fortunate to have highly visible leaders who exemplify a kaizen culture, leaders that take great pride in finding problems.

I asked Mr. Fujio Cho if his mentor Taiichi Ohno—the man considered the father of TPS—had a clear theory in mind when he began the implementation of TPS. Mr. Cho answered, "No." He explained that Mr. Ohno had developed TPS through solving problems that Toyota faced at an early stage of the company—like the shortage of cash—in very practical ways, not theoretical at all, including lots of trials and errors.

Mr. Cho said that Mr. Ohno gave him and other executives difficult problems to solve. Ohno checked to see how much the executives thought things through and expanded their ideas to really solve an issue. Mr. Cho explained, "Mr. Ohno's whole attitude about improvement was such that he was always evolving his thinking to overcome *new* problems, to the point where he did not mind showing his operations to others because, by the time they implemented copied ideas, he would have already come up with better ideas."

*No one has more trouble than the person
who claims to have no trouble.*

— Taiichi Ohno

Mr. Ohno saw the identification of problems as a competitive advantage and the key competency required to master TPS. His TPS was the result of constant problem finding, constant problem solving, and constant improvement. Without an awareness of problems, no kaizen can occur; a manager who accepts two defects out of 10,000 parts will not be able to eliminate those two defects.

Make Finding Problems Your DNA

As Toyota expanded around the globe, its philosophies, kaizen culture, and problem-finding behaviors—*Toyota DNA*—became increasingly difficult to transfer to thousands of new managers and team members. Many earnest attempts were made to define Toyota DNA between 1987–2000. This was frustrating: documentation was scarce, and language and corporate barriers grew location by location. As it expanded, the company was not physically centralizing its facilities as it had in Japan. It went from having 10 plants within a 30-mile radius of Toyota City to far-flung plants around the globe.

The need within Toyota at that time and the problem to be solved was how to manage and guide people around the world, presenting a single system of what a Toyota person is and what they must do—find problems and solve problems anywhere. But, with expansion, the Toyota DNA was diluted. How could we communicate it outside of Japan? How could we make people believe in problem finding and solving? How could management provide the methodology and establish the systems to reveal or create problems?

Mr. Cho, president of Toyota, and his staff—including me and my Georgetown colleagues, Tak Hata and Hiro Yoshiki—wrote *The Toyota Way 2001*. The purpose of the document was to preserve and articulate Toyota DNA and to emphasize the need for further development. It describes how people at Toyota should act on a daily basis (i.e., common culture) in order to achieve Toyota business goals.

For the first time, Toyota corporate culture was codified and organized in a way that could make it globally applicable. While most Western managers at the time were learning about TPS and its tools, Toyota was instead looking to communicate and clarify its culture. In fact, only about one page of the 14-page document addresses lean systems and structures (i.e., TPS).

The Toyota Way 2001 describes the two essential pillars—continuous improvement and respect for people—that are the core of Toyota DNA. Within these two pillars, five supporting concepts must exist for problem finding and problem solving to flourish. A successful company also needs to have a shared vision that, when unmet, presents a problem for all in the organization to find. An inspirational vision challenges people to take calculated risks with little fear of failure because of the valuable lessons learned in the process of trying to find and solve a dynamic problem and continuously improve.

Toyota's guiding vision: better cars for more people.

For years, the guiding vision was simply to provide better cars for more people. At its inception, Toyota sought to make a car affordable for the ordinary Japanese citizen. Given that they were without any auto manufacturing experience or a supporting auto supplier base, the dream was ambitious and executives found many problems. Since then, top Toyota executives repeatedly create additional bold visions and challenge Toyota management to find associated problems.

From the day I joined Toyota in 1970, I received clear direction from President Eiji Toyoda, the most influential executive in Toyota history. He declared a vision for Toyota to be an independent auto company with the world's third largest production volume (2 million) in the 1970s and 10 percent of the global automotive market share (equivalent to No. 1 in the world) in the 1980s. Prior to 1972, the Japanese auto industry had been protected by the government. Mr. Toyoda reasoned in the early 1960s that only a larger, stronger Toyota could fend off acquisition by one of the US's Big Three automakers.

This vision surfaced many problems that stood in the way of Toyota being competitive in the world: the lack of size, products, and human resources; inadequate quality and efficiency; and the lack of a comprehensive management system. He posed the vision, and management found and solved the problems:

- New plants and new products
- Management system based on PDCA, including hoshin planning/vision deployment system
- Training system to develop human resources
- Quality-control system based on statistical process control
- Product-export effort to grow the size of the company
- Production system (TPS).

Almost every system Toyota enjoys today was developed in response to the vision of Eiji Toyoda, and the problems that it presented to management. Ohno developed TPS in response to this vision. Mr. Toyoda had given him a problem to solve.

Hiroshi Okuda, Toyota chairman from 1996–2001, identified environmental issues due to global warming as a growing problem for the auto industry and for companies that addressed it a competitive advantage. At the time, Toyota had no technical advantage in green vehicles. Thus Mr. Okuda's vision created a problem and a challenge—a Toyota vehicle with double the fuel efficiency in three years. That challenge resulted in the Prius. The chief engineer of the Prius, Takeshi Uchiyamada, later became the company's chairman.

Visions such as these create conditions by which executives in an organization can assess the current condition and see how it relates to the vision. Toyota defines the gap between the current status and either an established standard or ideal status as a problem. Is there a problem that prevents your organization from moving closer to its vision? Of course there is. Your challenge is to find it, clearly understand it, and then attack it.

As you and your management team find problems, explore ways to solve problems, and incrementally improve the organization (kaizen) toward a shared vision, you will gradually develop a sense that this is normal behavior—a kaizen culture emerges. Everyone is compelled to find problems and pursue improvement, innovation, and evolution of their work, as opposed to hiding problems and maintaining the status quo. Mr. Okuda would express his frustrations, saying, "Without organizational efforts, kaizen will not continue, and doing and changing nothing may prevail. You should regard doing nothing and changing nothing as the worst thing to be done. The existence of a strong company culture that drives status quo will ruin the company."

Lean systems and structures, as described in *The Toyota Way 2001*, helped everyone within the company find problems. Toyota executives, including Mr. Okuda, believed it was necessary to share current conditions visually and transparently across the organization, and to do so in a way that they could be evaluated relative to standards, targets, or plans. Everyone must clearly recognize a problem when they see it and have a sense of urgency to solve the problem when found.

It is important here to note a belief of Mr. Okuda that is absolutely necessary for problem finding and improvement in your organization to take hold: Those who find and take on difficult problems but fail should be praised as long as organizational lessons are learned from the failure. *Finding the problem* was the greater challenge. Finding and solving problems—using the solution, such as a more efficient process, as a new standard, which then surfaces additional problems—is an endless cycle of improvement.

How do you really know that a seeming problem is the real problem? Every day someone in your company tells you about a problem they have or the company has. How many of those are really problems that prevent your company from achieving its shared vision? It might not be a problem, or it might only be a problem that is important to one manager. The only sure way to separate the two is going to the source to find the facts. (Management by facts is what Toyota means by *genchi-genbutsu*).

Not having the facts leads to speculation. Debating without verified facts is speculation. Management based on speculation, hearsay, or gut beliefs almost always leads to wrong decisions and/or delayed solutions. Differing opinions (not facts) disrupt cooperation and delay finding and solving the real problem. Improvement efforts attack the wrong problem because it was not confirmed with facts. They don't drive all the way the root cause confirmed with facts.

> *Of course we like data. But I prefer facts.*
> — Taiichi Ohno

You and your management should make it a practice to go and see the important facts for yourselves or, at a minimum, request staff to "go and see" and report on key issues; you will then confirm the key issues. This produces two good outcomes: staff develop their skills with genchi-genbutsu, and management receives the facts they need to clarify the problem.

Mr. Ohno epitomized management by facts and often went to the plant floor to confirm a fact. He was once troubled by a surprising improvement of a crankshaft line that had repeatedly had problems delivering on time. He was given data about the improvement, but he wanted the facts. How had this sudden improvement occurred? How could it be emulated elsewhere?

Carefully examining the line, he realized that a manager had secretly built and hidden excess safety stock to cover up for the line's habitual delivery problems. Mr. Ohno was, of course, furious that inventory was being increased rather than the real problem solved, and decided to take dramatic action. He ordered employees to bury the excess stock on the plant grounds. After he gave his order and left, the manager persuaded employees to again hide the excess. It didn't take long for Mr. Ohno to find the excess stock once again, and this time he ordered it destroyed before his eyes.

One day at Toyota Motor Manufacturing Kentucky (TMMK), a junior manager told me that everyone complained about our pension plan. "Tell me, who *everyone* is?" I responded. His answer was that three managers had expressed their concern over the pension—but he had not asked hourly team members or non-managers about the plan. I told him, "You must tell me then that three managers complained about the pension, not everyone."

We later discovered through an internal survey that managers who had come from the Big Three automakers were unhappy with our pension, but the majority of hourly team members and managers were satisfied. Additional market data indicated that we might need to improve salaried pensions to be comparable with the auto industry, but that our pensions were competitive with other industries. We also knew of the problems associated with the Big Three pension plans, which were lavish but unfunded. Based on all of these *facts*, we made appropriate adjustments in our salaried pensions that saved significant money without hurting the morale of hourly team members.

Respect for people (respect and teamwork)

Respect for people is rooted in the belief that continuous improvement will secure the prosperity of both an organization and its employees. It also is based on the belief that the ability of human beings is infinite if they are respected, developed, and inspired. When people are inspired to move toward a shared vision, they can be a formidable force.

However, if a company does not *respect* its employees and stakeholders—customers, business partners, stockholders, people in the community—they will not support the company and continuous improvement will never happen. Individuals and suppliers will not look for problems if only the company benefits from finding and solving problems. Respect is a two-way street. For example, suppliers will not share cost-cutting ideas with customers if the customers benefit but do not share savings with or make commitments to suppliers. Workers will not contribute improvement ideas if they believe they'll lose their jobs as the result of efforts that reduce labor for a process.

At NUMMI, we were eventually offered many improvement ideas by the UAW members once we showed them examples of kaizen activities that had occurred in Japan and how this process positively impacted their job security. We listened to the ideas of Fremont employees on how to solve problems in their operations, and the UAW members were eager to put their ideas in action to build better quality vehicles and improve productivity. It was easy to see that most workers took pride in their jobs and got

The Role of Lean Systems and Structures in Finding Problems

The following lean systems and structures are key to finding and solving problems and continuous improvement (kaizen):

• *Regard for next process* (just-in-time system): Every process must produce in a satisfactory way the amount that the next process (internal customer or end customer) needs, or produce only the amount consumed by the downstream operation. This enables operations to hold minimum inventory, which has obvious benefits, but it also means the process must be highly predictable in order to meet customer demand. When there is a problem with the process, problems are quickly noticed because there is a stoppage of the operation in the downstream process, and the problems are rapidly addressed because they jeopardize delivery to the customer. Ideally, they also are fixed permanently to prevent a reoccurrence.

• *Revealing problems* (jidoka system): Jidoka—automatic abnormality detection—shuts down an operation once it detects an abnormal situation (a problem) in the process. By employing jidoka, management has a system to detect abnormality at the point of occurrence, like andon, or a dashboard to pinpoint the trouble operation, and is alerted to problems that require quick action to fix (if only temporarily) and deeper problem solving skills to prevent a reoccurrence.

• *Elimination of waste* (muda): Finding wastes (problems) and eliminating them reduces costs and improves profits. Instead of raising the price to improve profitability, cost reduction is a more secure way for improved profit. Educating people to look for waste is the tool to develop problem finders everywhere. Toyota's famous seven wastes were developed for this purpose, and they fall into two categories. The first category (waiting time, non-essential conveyance, unnecessary processing, and non-value-added motion) is easy to understand but difficult to detect. For example, one can appear busy without getting much done, which is a problem. The second category (over-production, excessive inventory, and defect correction/rework) is more difficult to understand and practice but easy to detect because you can see these wastes on the floor or warehouse. The key for improvement in the second waste category is to set ambitious targets, like a 50% reduction of inventory, which will assuredly surface problems and, thus, cause management to question common practices and experiment with new ideas.

- *Elimination of overburden* (muri): Finding overburden problems and eliminating them reduces errors, defects, and injuries. Overburden leads to hurried behavior, excessive overtime, and/or ergonomically unhealthy postures and habits that can cause mistakes, cause individuals to overlook defects, and result in injury. Line supervisors and a manager should be educated and trained to find overburden on the production floor and in the office.

- *Elimination of unevenness* (mura): Unevenness or instability is a big and thorny problem. Management must be educated and trained to find problems of this type, using tools such as the material and information flow chart. When mura occurs in production scheduling, one operation is idle but another is busy, and management has to deploy excessive people to meet the fluctuation. To eliminate unevenness, Toyota adopted the leveled scheduling technique (heijunka). If mura occurs in information flow, workers are forced to wait until necessary information is in their hands and are likely to be overburdened when the information finally becomes available. This is a typical problem in an office as well as on the production floor.

satisfaction by making improvements. I came to realize that NUMMI members wanted to be respected.

I remember one worker who was one of the older union leaders. He took a device from his pocket and told me that he could install a glass window in almost half of the allocated time. He told me that he regularly employed this practice so he could spend the rest of the assembly time reading, a habit developed when GM ran the plant. I watched as he applied the device into the door panel to guide glass to the exact position. The device was so effective and the process repeatable by others—not just this one clever member—that it was adopted into every Toyota operation, including plants in Japan.

At the beginning of my contract negotiations for NUMMI, the concepts of mutual trust and mutual responsibility were uncommon to UAW officials. They thought it was just a slogan. We carefully spelled out mutual responsibilities for each party, which we believed could lead to a state of mutual trust—not a given condition but rather something to be earned through the mutual efforts by all parties. (See Appendices: *Mutual Trust and Responsibilities at NUMMI*.) The more evidence of mutual responsibility, the more confidence in the other parties, and as confidence grows conflict decreases, satisfaction increases, and benefits result. Eventually, mutual trust occurs.

The terms clarified everyone's responsibility in the joint venture, and it also recognized the need to support or assist each other while accomplishing each party's own responsibilities. For example, the UAW recognized the necessity of productivity increases and the need to promote constant improvement in quality and productivity.

Meanwhile individual employees had a responsibility for kaizen to make the company more productive, and the company, in turn, had the responsibility to keep them employed and improve wages and benefits. Given this kind of trust in which each

Developing People Requires Trust

One Toyota maxim is that if a leader has not developed their staff to a skill level equal or superior to their own, then the supervisor should not be promoted—the team would be weakened by their departure because no one would be able to take their place. Developing people is an ongoing process that involves a continuous sharing of knowledge and skills between managers and employees who trust each other.

party fulfilled their responsibilities sincerely and supported and expected others to carry out their responsibilities, NUMMI achieved its goals from the outset.

To maximize the potential of the organization, we also needed to *develop each individual member* and *foster teamwork*. One innovative individual or a strong leader might influence change, but without teamwork it will never be sustained. Team members will not buy into a decision if they don't trust the leader, and they cannot follow the decision if they lack the capability to do so.

Senior management is simply a flag-bearer when a business decision is made. It is of no use unless others follow.

— Eiji Toyoda

Looking Ahead

In the following chapters we will describe some systems and techniques to establish a kaizen culture and problem-finding behaviors in your organization. They will help you to find and solve problems by motivating and reinforcing behaviors that drive problem solving and continuous improvement—breaking large, complex problems into addressable issues; and creating problems to overcome complacency.

All of the approaches are necessary for leaders to achieve and sustain lasting kaizen. Many organizations that have pursued lean probably recognize the basics of problem solving. Or maybe your organization eventually achieved kaizen but could not sustain it. At Toyota too, an *all-is-well* attitude would occasionally seep back into the company culture. Considering how quickly some industries change and how rapidly performance benchmarks are raised. Such contentment, even for a brief period, can put a company at a huge competitive disadvantage.

Chapter 1 Key Questions

- Does your organization have a vision that will require problem finding and problem solving from all employees and stakeholders—senior leadership through plant floor members—to achieve?

- Do your employees respect and trust management enough to take the initiative to reveal and solve problems?

- Do you and other leaders in your organization always rely on facts for decision-making, or do you occasionally trust your instincts, intuition, or unsubstantiated opinions?

- Have you built in the systems (e.g., JIT, jidoka) that routinely force awareness and resolution of problems?

- Does your organization have a kaizen culture?

2. Develop Problem Solvers

Georgetown

I n March 1986, when I set foot in Georgetown, Kentucky, it was a farm town. There were about 20,000 people in all of Scott County, best known for its horse-breeding industry. I was the first Toyota employee in Kentucky. My role was to staff a plant from the ground up. That meant establishing a new human-resources organization and HR systems and find all American managers, as well as 2,000 production employees, and 300 skilled trades to join me there. I also faced the rare challenge of trying to replicate in the Georgetown greenfield the Toyota kaizen culture, which had taken Toyota Japan a half-century to nurture. How would I establish a management team and workforce capable of endless improvements in this bucolic but remote setting?

Gathering a Toyota Workforce

The Georgetown groundbreaking ceremony was in May 1986, and soon thereafter Toyota built an assembly plant, stamping shop, and a plastics-molding shop (the first such shop outside of Japan for Toyota). Just as Toyota had blueprints for the buildings it would construct, I also had been developing a blueprint for an ideal Toyota workforce, one that with training and support would religiously embrace Toyota business practices and TPS and continuously find problems and improve the organization. My vision was to create the type of workforce that had gradually evolved in Japan through decades of problem finding under the guidance of famous leaders and business innovators. The most difficult aspect, I believed, would be to establish the same level of mutual trust and respect that had formed between Toyota employees and leadership in Japan.

We started by selecting a workforce which had the potential to fit into this vision and meet Toyota expectations. In order to receive incentives from the state, Toyota agreed to hire only Kentuckians for the production jobs; fortunately, we had 100,000 applicants for the initial 2,000 jobs. This allowed us to select team members based on an ideal profile of a team member and someone who was compatible with our system: individuals with a capacity to understand and analyze data, dexterity and stamina for repetitive production, quality consciousness, team-oriented behavior, a good work ethic, and a kaizen, problem-solving mind.

To identify the desired characteristics, the state checked cognitive abilities of applicants, and we developed an assessment center with Development Dimensions International (DDI) to assess physical and behavioral requirements. As a result, we not only hired highly educated and motivated team members, but we also were able to establish a standard hiring process that went above and beyond legal requirements. This selection system became the norm for Toyota outside of Japan, and the Big Three automakers followed this example in an effort to replicate our work environment.

Applicants' production skills or experiences generally were not considered critical factors for new hires; our intent was to develop a versatile and flexible workforce with a single job classification for production team members. New production members would learn all they needed to excel in that position through on-the-job experiences. We wanted a Toyota production employee, and simply did not care if he or she had been someone else's production employee. It didn't matter if a candidate was a specialized painter, welder, assembler, inspector, molder, machine operator, or driver.

The majority of people we hired had at least a high school diploma or equivalent, and 14% of our production team members had college degrees. This gave us a foothold to promote people from within and was critical for growing mutual trust. (See Appendices: *Georgetown New-Hire Education Profiles*.) Cheryl Jones was one example. Cheryl was a 25-year-old female supermarket manager for a supervisor role—an assembly line group leader—who went on to become a vice president in manufacturing. Similarly, Will James, an African American was hired to the facility as a group leader in 1987 and became president at the Georgetown plant in 2010.

For skilled team positions, such as maintenance, we did more advanced testing of skills and knowledge, but were unable to identify enough qualified candidates for the positions. So we instead hired engineers with associate degrees as well as selected production members who were willing to go through a 30-month training program to become a multi-skilled maintenance team member. These employees not only were required to keep equipment up and running at all times, but they would be used to support production team members and train them on daily maintenance tasks.

Unlike production members, managers were recruited from other automakers and were required to learn how to manage within the TPS environment. In hindsight, this was a serious flaw in my approach. Not because they could not or would not do the job, but because most of the manufacturing managers left the company when they were offered significantly higher salaries elsewhere because of their experiences in Georgetown. We learned our lessons from this experience and committed to promoting managers from within. We also did this with line supervisors, who grew up learning the Toyota system in-house and became its biggest advocates. Eventually the managers became pure Toyota leaders who had grown up in Toyota's system.

Training and Education

I met every new hire during an assimilation stage, and personally introduced them to our culture: e.g., kaizen mind, problem-finding and problem-solving attitude, teamwork, and fact-based management. But this was merely the beginning of Toyota's training and development process.

We sent production group leaders and team leaders to Japan for training, as we did at NUMMI, except we sent more

Georgetown people to be trained and increased the training period by one week to four weeks to make up for their lack of auto-manufacturing experience. Surprisingly, compared to NUMMI members, they learned key elements in half of the planned time and, thus, had more practice time in Japan. In some ways, they did better because, without previous auto-making experience, they did not doubt or question what their trainers told them.

In Kentucky we offered extensive classroom training to all the new hires. (See Appendices: *Georgetown New-Hire Training Courses*.) We made 28 programs available to the team members (many modules were required), and we reserved 5% of their working hours for training. We also conducted 40 hours of voluntary (without pay) pre-promotion training for individuals seeking group leader or team leader positions for the second shift; classes included Job Instruction, Problem Solving, and Effective Meeting Facilitation. Approximately 800 of 1,000 team members applied for this voluntary training in 1987. By October 1990, there were 3,463 production employees in Georgetown (which included 400 for a power-train plant that was added), of which 2,298 were team members.

Through the overall 28-course regimen, Georgetown team members were equipped with the basic knowledge of TPS and Toyota business practices. The number of training hours we conducted for initial team members was impressive.

- In 1990 alone, we trained 4,163 course participants a total of 103,793 hours (the equivalent of nearly 12 years)
- Assimilation: 523 participants and 16,736 hours
- TPS: 2,140 participants and 24,760 hours
- Employee development: 791 participants and 12,473 hours
- Skilled trades: 580 participants and 46,400 hours
- Management seminars: 128 participants and 3,424 hours

Belief in Toyota

The vision for Georgetown was to develop a workforce that would buy into Toyota practices. Prior to product launch in 1988, we had developed company policies and objectives, a kind of vision and mission describing how the Americans and Japanese should work together:

Basic philosophy

- Produce America's No. 1 quality car based on "customer first" philosophy.
- Contribute to the quality of life as well as the economic growth in the communities it serves.
- Promote stable employment and improved well-being of employees through growth of the Company.
- Develop a unique, innovative production and management system by combining the best ideas of two countries.

Operating principles

- Promote cost savings effort.
- Promote kaizen and team member participation.
- Promote team members' personal development.
- Promote open communication and encourage a free-flowing exchange of information.
- Work as a team with mutual trust and respect and with equal opportunities for all.
- Establish effective work practices and principles.
- Promote pride of workmanship.
- Maintain safe work environment.
- Develop a close working relationship with Toyota Motor Sales.
- Join other Toyota organizations to grow as a team.
- Develop a friendly relationship with the community.

Company Objectives

• Exceed Toyota plants in Japan in quality and cost of products.

• Nurture suppliers and establish good relations.

• Become profitable as soon as possible.

• Build a flexible organization to respond to various changes.

We aimed high from the very beginning; we wanted to produce America's No. 1 quality car and exceed Toyota plants in Japan in terms of quality and cost. These targets would never end because of competition among all car makers and plants. To achieve that, we would develop a flexible work environment, one in which kaizen was exercised, people were developed, teamwork was promoted, and cost was contained. This was done in a manner that everyone knew was for the sake of both company and team members—mutual trust and respect..

With the exception of a few recalcitrant managers, we were successful with staffing. Even in dealing with these managers, we uncovered techniques that would help create a better work environment for future managers and other employees: First we used one-on-one training for managers with assigned coordinators, who were required to develop the managers and those being groomed for managers through day-to-day interaction on their jobs. Managers and future managers could go to them as they would go to a teacher, with questions or when simply frustrated by TPS.

Because Toyota Japan did not have detailed requirements to be a manager, we created a document that spelled out Toyota's five management requirements and defined what a local manager must accomplish. Managers often felt that they could run their operation by themselves without the help of their Japanese coordinators, but I disagreed. They were failing to grasp problems like kaizen requirements and the organizational-development aspects of their role.

The job of the manager at the Georgetown facility was to control the results and lead the effort of the unit through five basic activities:

1. Following the Plan-Do-Check-Action control cycle to guide the unit to achievement of its planned result.

2. Seeking kaizen opportunities in the Plan-Do-Check-Action process to guide the unit to better results.

3. Motivating and developing individuals and the organization to higher performance.

4. Communicating openly and effectively in the unit and within the organization to promote good job relations.

5. Acquiring sufficient knowledge of the role and operation of the unit to demonstrate practical understanding of its work.

Successful performance of the activities of the Georgetown management requires several management dimensions in each area of activity. The requirements and dimensions were jointly decided upon by Japanese and local management in Georgetown, and we further defined them for managers. We then evaluated managers' progress toward these characteristics, and local managers realized that they had long way to go to fulfill their roles. The management requirements eventually evolved into a global evaluation system for all of Toyota. (See Appendices: *Required Management Abilities Developed in 1990.*)

Georgetown Results

We had developed a vision for the ideal Toyota employee, hired such individuals, and then assimilated them to the Toyota way of thinking and working. In May 1988, two years after the groundbreaking and precisely as planned, the first Camry rolled out of Georgetown. The plant was on its way to becoming the benchmark for the auto industry and had won five J.D. Power awards for the first six years operation under President Fujio

Cho's leadership. Team members were proud of their growth and accomplishment, and enjoyed better careers, compensation, and benefits as the company prospered. (With this success, I left Georgetown in1993. Mr. Cho left Georgetown a year later, after seven years of the most rewarding experience.)

During those initial years, the vast majority of Georgetown employees grew to trust this way of working, and the plant's Japanese leadership grew to trust and rely on them. I think that even Toyota leadership was surprised at the initial success and the level of quality and productivity—nearly on par with the mother plant in Tsutsumi, Japan. As important, the assimilation and training programs developed in Georgetown became the basis for the North American Production Support Center. The center was established in 2005 to promote the self-reliance of Toyota plants in North America, helping other Toyota plants and other manufacturers to pursue the Toyota way of endless improvements.

Develop Problem Solvers

The success of all manufacturing plants comes down to the people and people systems of those facilities. Even those that rely heavily on automation and machines are still run, maintained, and improved by people. Because of this, human-resources advocacy is critical to continuous improvement. Even with the concepts and systems Toyota used to guide and challenge the organization toward problem-finding and kaizen, efforts will eventually fail if the workforce is not nurtured, reward, retained, and made to feel as if every individual is as important as the corporation.

Even the best-laid plans for endless problem finding, problem solving, and improvement will eventually fail if a workforce believes that their efforts and improvements won't further their job security, their careers, and their lives. And if a workforce ever imagines that improvements will directly lead to job losses, the system will dramatically fall apart.

Employees need tangible assurances of their future; HR establishes those assurances. HR develops systems and techniques to motivate management and the workforce toward a state of continuous improvement and communicates and reinforces philosophies that drive a spirit of problem finding and kaizen. Without job security and mutual trust that such systems provide, employees won't discuss problems. They won't enjoy solving problems. They won't look for problems. No problems, no kaizen.

Michikazu Tanaka, former TPS leader at Daihatsu Motor Co. Ltd., talked about Mr. Ohno's real interest in manufacturing management: "What became clear during my work with Ohno-san is that his chief interest was something other than reducing work-in-process, raising productivity, or lowering costs. His ultimate aim, I gradually learned, was to help employees assert their full potential. And when that happens, all those other things will occur naturally."[1]

1. Koichi Shimokawa and Takahiro Fujimoto, *The Birth of Lean* (Cambridge, MA, Lean Enterprise Institute. 2009).

I rose to senior leadership at Toyota from an HR role, which helped me to learn, recognize, and communicate the importance of the HR function and people development in cultivating a problem finding, kaizen culture, and to help organizations achieve and sustain kaizen culture in both union and non-union settings. Because of the power of unions at Toyota plants in Japan and the highly restrictive union environment throughout that country, the HR function was a necessary and strong part of developing kaizen culture. Early in my career, I was frequently called to assess work conditions and issues raised by the union, and in doing so, repeatedly touched all facets of Toyota production. At Toyota, individuals in HR were planners and strategists of people resources; it was our job to create secure work environments of mutual trust in which kaizen could flourish.

HR had a strong role in Toyota's success: we improved the work of the members (neither appeasing nor battling them) while satisfying corporate goals (in contrast to labor relations departments in many companies where the objective is to win the contract war). I truly appreciated the role that unions played at Toyota. Union leadership brought union members' views to our attention, and they conveyed our views to the members. Union leadership has to make a sound case to members for them to agree upon issues with the company, just as any company should make the case to employees of its intentions. I always tried to provide the reasoning behind our counterproposals to the union's demands so they could confidently explain them to their members. I faced the UAW at NUMMI in the same manner.

By working many long days developing the Letter of Intent and the contract for NUMMI, I came to the conclusion that regardless of a union presence or not—which was up to members to decide—HR plays a critical role in motivating people to engage in kaizen and problem finding and make sure that labor is not treated as replaceable resources. Through my work at the non-union environment in Georgetown, I saw that HR (in the absence of unions) must protect a non-union workforce: establish mandates for job security, provide personal development, ensure adherence to standards, collect suggestions and grievances, provide access to information, provide rewards and incentives, and be an advocate for the employee. For example, early on we took away managers' authority to fire or discipline people, to eliminate the fear of repercussions against those who identify problems.

With or without unions, HR needs to be an advocate and not just an administrator, encouraging people to find and speak freely about problems and helping them to trust that their actions will benefit the company and themselves.

In Georgetown we were able to select the workforce with which we wanted to work. That probably is not available to you as you look to build a kaizen culture. But that advantage was only a small part of our success. Three other key concepts will enable you and your leadership team to develop a culture of endless improvement:

- People development

- Self-motivated learning and problem-finding

- Environment of mutual trust and respect

People Development

In the US and Europe, achievement and performance often are all that is required for promotion. Managers or supervisors too often are concerned about *their* performance and think that tying their fortunes to others via training and mentoring could eventually put their own jobs in jeopardy. This environment is encouraged by companies, intentionally or unintentionally: these same supervisors were probably hired as qualified, experienced individuals and expected to do their jobs on Day One and then move up through the ranks as quickly as possible.

This approach emphasizes the individual. But for problem finding and kaizen to flourish, the emphasis must be on the good of the team serving the good of the company. The emphasis on team requires development of all on the team.

In contrast, Toyota usually hired job candidates from schools or the general labor market without specific credentials to do a job immediately because the company could then develop them in the best interest of the team. In other words, the team developed the newcomer to fit into their way or team culture, making the team stronger. If a team member failed to perform well, the supervisor for the team was blamed and not the team member. It was a development issue, not a capabilities problem.

I graduated from the University of Tokyo with a law degree in 1970 and immediately joined Toyota Motor Corporation in Toyota City, along with three others who had the exact same educational background. None of us was assigned to the legal department; I landed in Labor Relations, and the others in Personnel, Asset Management, and Information Technology. After our initial assignments, we rotated through various departments to acquire different knowledge and experiences.

This was typical of people development at Toyota in Japan. Most new hires, with or without college degrees, were assigned to an entirely different field from their education background. With the exception of a few job classifications (e.g., engineering), new employees did not join the company for a specific job. Toyota placed higher value on practical on-the-job business experience than the knowledge acquired in an academic setting or another company. Toyota sought to develop expertise based on demonstrated capability and job fit through rotation after hiring.

Toyota emphasized that educating and developing team members was a supervisor's most important job. If a supervisor had not developed staff to the level as equal or better then their own, then they would not be promoted to a higher level—even if they had achieved other business goals. With no one qualified to take their place, the team would be weakened if the manager was promoted.

In addition, college graduated team members rotated jobs every three to five years and worked with various supervisors who also rotated. Thus, the team members felt that they are working for the company, rather than an individual boss that they must impress. They were also more likely to respect their bosses as teachers and mentors throughout their careers.

The concept of hiring as a trainee instead of being hired for a specific job is a good practice that can work in the US or Europe, as was demonstrated at Georgetown. As you consider how to train managers and staff for your culture, keep your development systems focused on the following objectives:

- *Vision-oriented:* Educate people to share your vision and challenge them to buy into/strive for this vision. Build competencies respective to their roles (e.g., teamwork as a member, people development as a supervisor, challenging spirit as a leader) that will allow them to move their team toward your vision.

- *Problem-specific*: Provide people with skills or knowledge to improve those aspects of their work life that prevent them from attacking bigger problems. For example, the rotation method allowed individuals to learn problem-solving approaches from many different supervisors, which rounded out employees' abilities and enabled them to progressively tackle bigger, more complex problems.

- *Job-based*: Classroom training typically should be confined to introductory learning. On-the-job practice of what is taught in the classroom is essential and imperative to master skills, and this should ideally occur under a supervisor's coaching or in a manner that the supervisor can monitor outcomes. Toyota always asked participants in a problem-solving class to bring their problems from the job to the class after they have agreed upon the problem with their supervisors. This further connects the classroom training with supervisors, who are expected to coach the participant, regardless if they are a team member or a manager, on how to solve an agreed-to problem on site.

At Toyota Japan there are many programs and departments designed to impart lifelong, on-the-job training for employees, such as Toyota Institute for business practices or problem solving, Global Production Center for manufacturing know-how and skills, Operation Management Development Division for TPS, and TQM Promotion Division for business process development. The Team Member Development Center did the same in North America. The objective of these departments is to help members believe in the Toyota vision and the systems to achieve the vision.

Unless your education and development programs make people believers of your vision and systems, it will not work. The North American Team Member Development Center stated, "A Toyota team member is a person who can use problem-solving skills effectively." In other words, if you cannot do this, you are not (yet) a Toyota person. We wanted employees to be one with the company. If they cannot make this connection, they will eventually tire of finding problems and making improvements and take their learning somewhere else.

Self-Motivated Learning and Problem-Finding

To achieve a state of endless improvement, an organization must leap from management-driven improvements to employee-driven improvement, particularly for none-exempt employees who have less opportunity to challenge existing practices and performance. Employees must be motivated to learn, seek out, and solve problems on their own. You need ways to organize that environment and to promote individual initiative for learning and problem finding. We have repeatedly found great value in quality circles, suggestions systems, and, most of all, the use of incentives and job security for those who buy into the vision and leverage the systems in place to improve themselves and the organization.

Quality circles

Quality circles (QC) usually consist of a small, voluntary group of problem solvers that meet occasionally to tackle large problems. Because employees discuss and analyze problems as a group, they are more likely to fight to find a solution than if they had to go it alone. QC members have a common interest in the problem (shared value) and work at the problem for their own satisfaction.

QC members select their problem to be solved and its target to be achieved as a team, and they assign a role for each member to play. One individual may gather data, another track progress of the process, another solicit opinions at the gemba, another test countermeasures, etc. Through periodic meetings they find facts, drill down to a root cause through cause-and-effect analysis, and conduct trial-and-error experiments. They eventually come up with a solution to *their selected problem* and implement it to *their satisfaction*. Because participation in a QC is voluntary; members can drop off if they are no longer interested in the problem. That usually only happens once a problem has been solved.)

In a kaizen culture, QC members enjoy being challenged by the problems they select—as opposed to being challenged by a superior or working in an organization where their ideas and input are not valued. The problem-solving activities also offer them an opportunity to interact with leadership and other departments, furthering their learning about the company, its vision, and its systems, and getting them recognition as a potential leader.

Suggestion system

Would you rather have 100 grievances, or 100 grievances that are each accompanied by a suggestion? A group initiative, like quality circles, is not for everyone. Some employees prefer an opportunity to contribute as an individual. For this reason, a suggestion system should be used to solicit individual ideas that can improve operations.

To make the suggestion system work, you must generate enough interest to get as many ideas as possible. In baseball lingo, many of these ideas may only be singles or just advance a runner, but with more ideas the odds are greater that someone will hit a home run. To generate sufficient interest requires both monetary and non-monetary incentives.

The first, critical non-monetary incentive is acceptance of insignificant ideas. When an individual has a complaint about their job, allowing them to come up with suggestions and ideas to resolve their own complaint may provide a way to release their frustrations. For example, a member had suffered from back pain when installing parts into a car body. He suggested a safety improvement, such as a sliding chair, to support his posture. The supervisor thought the idea was silly and ignored it. The worker was disappointed, never suggested another idea, and later filed a workers' compensation claim for back pain. If the supervisor had recognized his idea (good or bad) and discussed further how to implement or improve upon it, such recognition might have prevented the claim being filed and also helped other workers suffering from the same physical condition.

We eventually took the idea of the sliding chair seriously and expanded upon it. Maintenance and production workers developed various types of sliding chairs to make many operations easier. As the result of easy access to vehicles and improved posture across the assembly line, we reduced injuries and improved productivity and the quality of parts installation.

A well-promoted and closely monitored suggestion system can transform people's negative energy of a problem into positive energy to create a solution. Management must encourage workers to offer up small ideas, regardless of how significant the improvement or impact may be. Don't immediately look for big ideas when the suggestion system is implemented. The first step is to have a successful system, which should be judged by the *number* of suggestions received, not the cumulative benefit of suggestions.

I once asked a few workers who each suggested more than one hundred ideas every year how they came up with so many ideas. They told me that it was easy because they found so many problems every day about their operation, material, conveyance, maintenance, etc., and they "wanted to complain" as well as solve the problems. Without this constructive format in which to voice their complaints, I am sure many of these employees would have been a bad influence on coworkers. They should be commended because they have a great eye on problems.

Another non-monetary incentive is quick implementation. We observed that if a member suggested an idea and was told by their supervisor that it was accepted, but then it was not implemented within than three months, the member would lose interest in the suggestion system and likely not offer any more ideas. When an idea is implemented quickly, it makes an employee proud of the change and they tell colleagues of the contribution. This is a critical moment of self-satisfaction and pride necessary for endless improvements.

Management must set aside time—their own, as well as for maintenance, engineering, administration, etc.—to promptly facilitate and implement ideas. You may think this will be too time-consuming, but it adds value by building trust and respect, and it pales in comparison to the time you would spend addressing grievances instead.

A suggestion system can be 90% successful with these two non-monetary incentives—acceptance of insignificant ideas and quick implementation. A monetary incentive can deliver the final 10%. Setting the precise payout from savings that suggestions deliver is a challenging decision and unique to every organization.

At Toyota, we did not think that bigger was necessarily better because, as noted, we encouraged small suggestions to improve the level of employee participation and dilute negative energy and complaints. But too small of a payout can discourage or anger workers and send the wrong message. Get employee input and clarify the payout-calculation formula in advance of implementing your suggestion system to get it off to a good start and to avoid any disputes that could arise, including who holds patent rights for ideas suggested.

Rewards and recognition

Leadership establishes a vision and sets the standards for processes and targets of the operation, and we organize people in teams to strive for these vision and targets. Are workers naturally inclined to find the problems and solve them for improvement? The answer is "no" for a majority of workers because they do not initially see advantages for them in doing so. The obvious reason is that if members initiate problem solving and improve productivity, surplus workers will be identified and cut. Workers will fear job loss and become reluctant to be involved. Only problems directly related to their benefit, such as safety or quality, may get attention. Others, like energy, material, scrap, and conveyance may be ignored.

Workers need incentives to change and to find and solve problems. We believe the most important incentive is job security. No one should be laid off as the result of improvements. This statement should be voiced prior to kaizen of any operation at any time, reassuring workers of their importance to the organization. Regardless of the type of improvements your organization seeks—

productivity, quality, safety—*regularly communicate that no one will lose their job because of an improvement.*

Some managers—maybe even you—will question why a company would invest time and money to improve an operation and then refuse to remove labor from that operation when it is no longer required. Indirectly, Toyota does shed labor, but it does so in a far more patient and positive manner: as improvements occur that require less staff, extra workers are transferred to new business or busier operations, or placed in open positions when someone quits or in areas with problems that require more staff.

In Georgetown, we took this no-layoff approach even further. We created a kaizen team policy, which stated that a manager should have a kaizen team to absorb extra workers as the result of productivity improvements. This was a team of offline workers to further improve operations, who returned to a line job when an opening occurred. The faster kaizen was done and an operation improved, the more people went offline to assist a manager with kaizen. Workers enjoyed the offline work, accumulated kaizen experience, and further developed their problem-solving skills. Managers appreciated the extra help to improve their operation, and were pleased they did not have to go to their boss for support. Furthermore, managers were able to recognize good performance by placing capable workers on the kaizen team, which was an incentive for workers to improve their performance.

As you can imagine, this became a virtuous cycle of kaizen and kaizen culture-building. In addition, workers who landed on the kaizen team frequently showed leadership capabilities, and were good candidates for team leader roles. Compare this to what would have occurred had we simply laid off workers for the quick cost reduction: no incentive for kaizen to occur, and, thus, no kaizen. The method may be slow to produce returns, but it will undoubtedly deliver more cost savings than cutting staff and, in the long run, will keep employee staffing at levels flexible and able to ramp up in a growing, thriving company.

Once workers are assured that they will have a job—even when improvements could warrant otherwise—the next necessary incentive is a monetary reward for their continuous improvement. Call it "gain sharing" or "distributing cost savings" or whatever works in your culture. The point is that people want some return from their kaizen efforts. Even with systems in place to drive problem finding and improve performance, the majority of managers and workers will eventually lose interest in continuous improvement because they do not want to do the additional work without a real, tangible reward.

Toyota Japan developed productivity-based cash allowances for everyone. The allowance was not based on an individual's performance but on a group performance. Members in a group were paid equally and the incentive promoted teamwork. In North America, we introduced monetary incentives, which reflected companywide performance for productivity, safety, quality relative to targets, and individual attendance. The incentive recognized individual contribution to a group's performance for six months. We allocated up to 15% of pay for the reward, which was paid out biannually as a lump sum.

The effects of the North American incentive system were not as clear as those in Japan, due in part to multiple key performance indicators (KPIs) in North America compared to one KPI in Japan (see Chapter 3 for more details). In North America, team members appreciated the payout and retained a positive attitude toward problem solving and continuous improvement. In that sense it did what it was intended to do. But there were always a few people who simply wanted a traditional worker's role, and these workers ended up benefitting from the incentive system without contributing on par with other employees.

Another incentive was promotion. Promotional opportunities were not offered to those who simply wanted a traditional worker's role. This incentive worked favorably for those with a positive attitude toward problem solving and continuous improvement.

In North America, most production management was promoted from within—production workers to management team. This had happened because almost all the production managers that were original hires in Georgetown were attractive recruitment targets.

Promotion and people development should go hand in hand. All training should align with the core requirements or competencies needed for members to perform their jobs. Every new assignment should initially be harder for them to perform than their prior role. Management and employees will want to learn more in order to succeed in these new roles. Thus, an endless cycle of personal improvement will occur alongside the path of operations improvement.

Mutual Trust and Respect

Mutual trust and respect between management and members is the most difficult condition to achieve but absolutely necessary to realize a flexible organization that will pursue continuous improvement forever. If management and team members do not trust each other, resulting in an adversarial relationship like that which existed between the Big Three automakers and the UAW for many years, there will never be real progress on any issue. Toyota learned this lesson as well after a bitter labor dispute with the union that drove Toyota to near-bankruptcy in the 1950s.

Having mutual trust exist within an organization is the ultimate milieu in lean management. You can sense when it really exists. It is like organizational overdrive, accelerating an organization toward its goal. Management uses the employees' time effectively, and employees relentlessly move the organization toward the greater value and toward greater self-satisfaction. It must be earned through mutual efforts to establish confidence that management and employees trust that both will try hard to discharge their own responsibility to each other for mutual benefit and satisfaction.

Mutual Trust at NUMMI

Prior to partnering with General Motors at the NUMMI plant in Fremont, CA, the facility was the epitome of an adversarial relationship. Employee grievances numbered in the thousands, and stories were rampant that workers intentionally sabotaged processes and products. Fremont under GM was the exact opposite of mutual trust.

We understood these problems coming in and through a rehiring process were able to select the best of the previous workforce, which gave us a promising start. The contract we forged with the UAW helped to move us toward mutual trust, spelling out our intent for workers "to gain from their labors a greater measure of dignity, self-fulfillment and self-worth." But it was a small yet meaningful lean tool that embodied the spirit of mutual trust for both management and employees.

The new Fremont management trusted members enough to let them pull an andon cord, which quickly illuminated that a problem existed and, not without consequence, stopped the production line (a stopped line can result in thousands of dollars of losses per minute). Management promised employees they would have the ability to stop the line if they encountered a problem, and management stuck to that promise. We told them that a member was responsible for pulling the andon cord to alert management of a problem, and the line would stop if the problem could not be fixed immediately. Workers then started trusting their bosses enough to ask for help by pulling the andon cord when there were problems. A team leader, who was a union member, would attempt to fix the problem before the situation warranted the line to stop.

Workers preferred the NUMMI system to the old combative one at GM. Many told us they enjoyed coming to work for the first time in their lives. One shop committeeman, who played an instrumental role in the contract negotiation, approached me after signing the contract. He said that because the plant really no longer needed the type of union protection that had been required, he would like to be a member of corporate employee relations to help NUMMI further develop mutual trust with the workforce. He switched his position from the union shop committee member to a labor relations representative for the company, and enjoyed his new job until he retired. Many old militant union leaders also became group leaders or line supervisors.

───────────────

The concept of mutual trust is foreign to many North American businesses *where leadership dictates* and *management and employees do*, and where eventually each side works against their adversary— either consciously (strikes, labor disputes) or subconsciously (punching in and leaving their minds at home). In such an environment, a problem-finding culture has no room to grow or be developed.

The following nine actions can help your leadership and management nurture a state of mutual trust and respect. Some actions are larger in scope and may require nominal investment and resources, but most reflect the Golden Rule[2] as it applies to management attitudes and behaviors:

1. Management should not avoid tough decisions

Mutual trust is not mutual dependency or blind acceptance by employees or management. Each party has a responsibility to the other. A big part of management's responsibility is a willingness to make decisions and then to be responsible for the outcomes of those decisions. Management runs the business as best possible for company success, trusting that employees will respond to policies with full and sincere communication. Management should listen carefully to employees' opinions because the key to a successful decision is that employees feel that management fully considered their input. This will help the decision gain acceptance and succeed.

2. Ethical code of reciprocity, often cited as "treat others as one you would like others to treat you."

But, ultimately, management must decide and take on the risks associated with their decisions. Employees, in turn, are expected to work hard and trust that management will make the right decision or correct it if it were a mistake. They should be able to believe that decisions are made to ensure long-term company prosperity and security for employees. This concept is backed by the principles and experience that only long-term company prosperity enables improved employment, wages, benefits, and job security.

2. Be honest

Management should be straightforward and open when sharing information with employees, such as business fundamentals (vision, mission, business conditions, long-term plans) to practical information (rules of conducts, organization changes, project news, business schedules, performances, expectations). Well-informed members are more likely to understand business decisions and support them, even if they don't totally agree.

For example, when Toyota reached an agreement with the UAW on how the transfer of individuals would occur at NUMMI, I went to the union hall to confirm that the union's understanding matched ours because the agreement was reached surprisingly quickly. I also offered renegotiation if their understanding was not the same. As I feared, there were minor misunderstandings, but the union was willing to go along with the agreement unless there was evidence that Toyota was abusing the policy. They surprised by my visit and appreciated my openness, especially when compared with the former GM labor-relations staff, which had tried to sneak company advantages into agreements.

After I moved on to Georgetown, I received a call from a NUMMI committeeman. Management and the union were trying to resolve a dispute regarding the same transfer clause and they asked for my interpretation. Even though my opinion favored the company, the committeeman accepted my interpretation because

Nine actions to help leadership and management nurture a state of mutual trust and respect.

1. Management should not avoid tough decisions

2. Be honest

3. Establish formal channels for management to share information and for employees to voice opinions

4. Keep promises

5. Be consistent and fair

6. Provide a conflict-resolution mechanism

7. Train employees

8. Provide stable employment

9. Provide proper rewards but save money for a rainy day

of the goodwill I had built with the shop committee and my honest sharing of information during my time at NUMMI.

While it should go without saying, I will say it nonetheless: supervisors, management, and leadership should never intentionally deceive an employee. Similarly, they should always represent their actions with employees in a true and honest light, never blaming employees for something they did not do nor taking credit for actions and ideas that they did not do or think.

Early in my career, one of my Toyota supervisors told his boss that my analysis had been wrong when his boss questioned a proposal I had written. The document had been reviewed and approved by my supervisor, so he shared in the responsibility for my analysis. It turned out that the analysis was correct, but my supervisor did not understand it well enough to answer his boss' question, and, thus, blamed me. So I had to go directly to my supervisors' boss for approval, and I lost all trust in my supervisor.

3. Establish formal channels for management to share information and for employees to voice opinions

Channels of communication are both large and small: The fundamental channel occurs regularly between a supervisor and employees. The supervisor needs the right information and the right amount of it to share. They should be trained to listen to employees and how to listen.

At the other end of the scale are management mechanisms, such as a company newsletter, a letter from the president to employees, and video broadcasts from senior leadership. These things occur within many companies for many reasons, but at Toyota, the intent was an honest sharing of information that everyone needed for continuous improvement. Before issuing any such broad communications, inform supervisors of what will be disseminated and prepare them to answer general questions about the content.

Lastly, establish formal means to capture employee opinions. One already outlined is a suggestion system. Another is an opinion survey to collect employees' voices and to better understand their needs and challenges. All results—favorable or not—from an employee survey must be shared with employees. Management must communicate how to improve the negative issues, as well as tell members what cannot be done, such as more wage increases than the company can afford.

At Georgetown, we spent time with each group reporting back survey results and letting members discuss internal issues they could improve in their group. We gathered the members' opinions about what actions we should take. From this feedback we made a Top 10 list of companywide issues and provided answers. We openly and honestly explained how we were going to improve some issues and why we could not address others.

Georgetown also had an anonymous hotline that members could call with complaints; answers to call-in issues were posted on bulletin boards across the plants. In a plant of more than 3,000 workers, these were very time-consuming activities. But they developed open dialogue among management and members and fostered the feeling that management was listening to members.

4. Keep promises

Some supervisors readily promise favors—increased wages, bonus, promotion, transfer—to get extra work out of employees. They may not do this with the intent to break the promise, but usually they don't deliver. Some will then go further and come up with an excuse for why the promise could not be kept, citing a budget or policy change.

This makes the company look untrustworthy. To prevent such irresponsible behavior, take away a supervisor's ability to use the carrot-and-stick approach. Tightly govern and thoroughly communicate how compensation, promotions, etc., are earned, leaving little doubt among employees what they must do to get what they want and deserve. Of course, senior leadership or any communicator or communication that represents the company must be held to this same basic standard.

I felt the most trust toward Toyota in 1974, after the first oil crisis. Toyota Japan had been telling members and its union that they would provide stable and gradual improvement in wages and benefits. A decade before the crisis, they had promised to pay and had been paying an annual bonus equivalent to 6.1-months of pay. Then the oil crisis hit the Japanese economy and Toyota hard, with both feeling the effects as early as 1973. Toyota profit had dropped by more than 80% from a year earlier.

Despite the difficult time, top management decided to pay the 6.1-month annual bonus because they knew the value of keeping their promise. Sure enough, team members were pleased and proud of the relationship with the company, and they worked hard to get through the economic crisis. Eiji Toyoda clearly said, "Employees should not be deceived" to emphasize the importance of sincere communication.

5. Be consistent and fair

Just as the manner in which employees perform their work is standardized, so too should the manner in which employees are treated, for good work behaviors or bad. Your company should present clearly defined rules and policies, that are consistently applied when dealing with employee issues. Employees should understand what they can and cannot do as a member of your organization. Anything other than this consistent approach quickly leads to an environment where favoritism is perceived, whether real or not.

Exceptions to the rules and policies, when necessary, should not be made by management or supervisors, but by the HR department. And like improving a standard, once an exception is made, determine if it should be incorporated into new rules and policies. HR should not be subject to the wishes of management or supervisors when determining treatment.

When employees can rely on the rules and policies and look to a central source of HR for explanations for exceptions, they will recognize fairness and consistent treatment and that the company is keeping its promises. Particularly when a company is evaluating an employee's performance, having a clearly defined standard of treatment with central oversight is crucial to build and sustain the trust of employees. As the central function, HR can compare the supervisors' evaluation and distribution of merit so as to keep consistency among them.

A manager once questioned me why we needed detailed rules of conduct, saying that no such rules are necessary because we trust employees. I told him that without rules and policies, management cannot expect employees to behave according to expectations, and employees would not know what to expect with regards to consequences of their conduct.

Being consistent also promotes fairness: Employees who do their job, pursue problem finding and kaizen, and dutifully follow rules and policies are rightfully treated differently than employees who under perform and/or subvert rules. If an environment develops where bad behaviors are not appropriately reprimanded as defined by the rules, then your good employees will feel that they have been unfairly treated, and their trust in the company will begin to erode.

6. Provide a conflict-resolution mechanism

In any organization, there will be conflicts that arise that are difficult to assess by the existing rules and policies. To deal with such issues, management should establish an objective conflict-resolution mechanism in order to rationally address the problem and diffuse any negative emotions associated with it—on the part of the employee or management. This mechanism should provide opportunity for full discussion and include an "umpire" to resolve the issue based on common sense.

When there was a conflict at Georgetown, we encouraged discussion between a manager and the team member involved, with an HR representative present as an employee advocate and to help them clarify and present their facts. If the parties could not resolve the issue, it was escalated to higher level, even up to the president. We also provided a peer review panel for serious issues, such as dismissals. The panel was composed of three randomly selected peers, two managerial staff, and an employee-relations manager as a facilitator. HR then decided the final outcome based on the recommendation of the panel.

The panel was sincere in their work and acted as a jury. Employee peers on the panel lauded their involvement and reported back to fellow members the fairness of the process and the fairness of the company.

In all the Georgetown cases that I recall, HR followed the recommendation of the panel, but they could and occasionally did alter the final treatment and conditions imposed if they had good cause. HR was not afraid of its responsibility to make decisions to foster mutual trust.

7. Train employees

In addition to all the benefits that training provides an organization in its quest for endless improvement, training affords employees the skills to do their jobs without detailed instructions or oversight. They see this as a sign of management trust, and in turn, typically will want to apply newfound skills to improve their role and the company.

Again, supervisors are on the frontline: determining what employees need day-to-day to do their jobs, ensuring that they are properly trained, and pushing them toward higher positions that will require more capabilities—and more training.

This sounds simple, but many times in a day a supervisor could more easily complete a task for an employee rather than train the employee learn about and complete the task. It is a constant balance between burdening employees with tasks that they are incapable of performing and supporting them in tasks that they are learning to perform.

8. Provide stable employment

No worker will improve their efficiency if they question their job security as a result of an improvement. At the very least, management must clearly and boldly assure job security as it relates to operations improvements. However, this presents issues of balance for management.

When demand is high, the tendency is to hire additional workers. But those new workers are subject to the same job security as long-time employees, and management should refrain from knee jerk hiring of extra employees at the first sign of need. Instead during high demand, ask employees to work overtime for a short period (three to six months, maximum) and to develop more capabilities, so that they can take on more responsibilities. In exchange for job security, people generally are willing to take on such challenges, particularly if they are afforded training and development opportunities.

At NUMMI, management and the union had agreed on a maximum mandatory overtime: two hours every day and two-thirds of a day on Saturdays. Georgetown had similar flexible overtime. Both conditions exceeded a normal UAW contract outside of Toyota.

In addition to flexible overtime, temporary employees should be utilized for short-term high demand or a temporary high load at certain jobs. But unlike what I see as a common practice, the temporary employees *should not* be utilized as a pool for new hires. They should be employees of an agency that staffs temporary non-core jobs that require little training and can be accomplished without sacrificing important values like quality. If not done in this manner, regular employees will perceive temporaries as new hires with unduly long-term probation periods, become sympathetic when these employees leave, and doubt management's intention to secure the jobs of employees.

As management avoids excess hiring and develops the work-force via the short-term measures described above, overall productivity is improved gradually and a minimum number of new hires are added to enhance long-term performance. Management builds more stable employment and employees become more valuable with continuous development, trusting the organization and enjoying their contributions to the company's success.

9. Provide proper rewards but save money for a rainy day

Management should provide proper rewards to members as company performance is improved, but also apply long-term thinking and save money for a rainy day. Group, member, and management rewards should be balanced with a cash reserve for capital investments, acquisitions, and expansions.

As the 2008 recession taught us, saving money can mean the difference between solvency and liquidation. After its near-bankruptcy experience in the 1950s, Toyota chose to save large sums of cash and eliminate reliance on financial institutions.

Having a large cash reserve created a huge advantage over the Big Three in recent decades. This no-debt condition was created by relentless cost savings by management and members, and has provided everyone with a sense of pride, ownership, and job security. As a result, Toyota's cost-consciousness spurred a culture of constant cost improvement amid an environment of stable employment. And management and members share the same value—mutual trust.

The nine considerations foster mutual trust, and all of these are requirements of management. Management has the authority to dictate to the whole organization what to do, how to do it, and where to go. Management should embrace these ideas and then enjoy employees' responses to their actions.

Employees will be motivated to pursue a true lean operation because they can trust management's decisions even though their own roles seem to continuously change for the sake of continuous improvement. They will enjoy their contribution toward the growth and prosperity of the company and for their own growth and prosperity.

Self-realization

Throughout my career I have seen and firmly believe that people will be addicted to pursue problems *for their own growth and self-realization* as long as there exists:

- An environment of mutual trust and respect between management and employees

- People development efforts by the company and supervisors

- Opportunities and support mechanisms that empower employees to solve problems

- Rewards for employee contributions.

People inherently want to believe in the vision and mission of their companies and of their workplaces. They want to contribute to and see progress toward a shared vision. They want to develop and grow as individuals, as they help their organization pursue a shared vision. When people reach this level of self-realization— be they supervisors, managers, specialists, or whomever—they literally cannot stop finding and solving problems because they enjoy it, it makes them feel confident, and to do otherwise would be denying themselves of pleasure and meaning.

I have seen countless individuals grow and evolve in this way. Individuals who reach a level of self-realization became missionaries of continuous improvement. They stimulate others and encourage the development of ever leaner systems in their places of work.

By contrast, many NUMMI people who returned to GM, or Georgetown people who left to pursue what they thought were better careers at other organizations, were disappointed with the new environments and the lack of a kaizen culture. They missed their former employers, and struggled to implement lean systems because there was no environment to support continuous improvement.

We are first and foremost individuals. As such, a belief in finding and solving problems and in a company's kaizen culture exists for our own satisfaction. We strive for endless improvement toward a shared vision because it makes us and our company unique.

Looking Ahead

Continuous improvement requires systems that educate, engage, and empower employees, and an active HR department that serves both management and the workforce. But even when management and the workforce are able to embrace a shared vision and systems are in place to inspire problem finding and solving, some problems will appear gigantic and insurmountable. You will learn in Chapter 3, that even the biggest problems can be broken down into manageable, solvable pieces. When problems are parsed and linked to roles and responsibilities that effectively engage management and members in identifying and solving them, almost any level of improvement is possible.

Chapter 2 Key Questions

- What role does HR in your company play in establishing and ensuring equitable application of employee development, reward/ recognition, and behavioral systems?
- Does your company have a no-layoff policy associated with kaizen/continuous improvement efforts? Why or why not?
- What mechanisms does your company have that promote self-motivated learning and problem solving among employees (e.g., suggestion system, quality circles)?
- Has your company fairly rewarded employees, supervisors, and management relative to individual and/or company performance? Why or why not?
- What level of trust and respect exist between frontline employees and supervisors and management? What has contributed to this current level (good or bad) of trust and respect?

3. Break Big Problems into Smaller Ones

Europe

Moving to the United States and leading the effort to get the NUMMI joint venture and Georgetown plant off the ground were challenging moments in my career: a new country, a new role, and a new language. But I was soon asked to take on a bigger problem at Toyota's Manufacturing operations in Europe, including the UK, France, Turkey, Poland, and Belgium.

In 2001, I was named the executive vice president of Toyota Motor Engineering & Manufacturing Europe (TMEM), located in Brussels. I was put in charge of production control, production engineering, accounting, finance, human resources, information systems, and corporate planning. Shuhei Toyoda, the third son of legendary Toyota chairman Eiji Toyoda, was appointed president.

Toyota's overall European operations had lost €2 billion in 2000, mainly due to significant losses on imported products, expensive cars, and parts from Japan due to the strong yen (approximately 100 yen to 1 euro). The manufacturing group of companies in Europe lost about €500 million.

Shuhei and I were given three years to turn things around and make Europe profitable. I had to clarify this unwieldy problem in the context of a long-term goal: "Turn European operations into the third pillar of global Toyota (joining Japan and North America), as defined by the Toyota 2010 vision and evidenced by sustainable profitability." This would require the entire European operation to make more than €1 billion in profits by 2010, with €600 million coming from manufacturing.

I had few clues to the underlying causes of this continental-sized problem. Surely, Toyota Japan management struggled to apprehend this matter clearly. Just before departing for Europe, President Cho called me into his office and told me to find the key problems in Europe and report back directly to him. At the time, I believed that solving these problems was beyond my capacity or even the capacity of our management team. It was, however, my responsibility to do this, and I knew of only one way: break down this giant problem into smaller—solvable—problems.

First, I split the profitability problem into: a revenue problem and a cost problem (profitability = revenue – cost). Second, the cost problem was further divided into current-product cost reduction and future product cost (cost planning). Third, I added three separate problem categories that contributed to the first three: people, organization, and risk.

Thus, the huge challenge had been broken down into six categories, which were further broken down into sub-problems (see Toyota's European Problem below). Each member of our management team, including the president, was responsible for at least one sub-problem. No one could say, "This is not my responsibility."

Toyota's European Problem—Not Profitable

Disunited organization	Insufficient revenue	Not enough cost reduction
Unclear roles and responsibilities	Low ex-factory price	Weak cost management
Lack of functions	Constrain on volume	Expensive diesel engine
Various stages of organization	Low volume of each model	High depreciation
Lack of direction/ hoshin management	Low local value-added	High logistics costs
Lack of decision-making system	Old products	Uncontrolled labor costs
Various IT systems	Too much sales support	
Duplicated administration		

It also was my responsibility to establish the systems for detecting new problems, monitoring problems with our problem-solving process, and sharing progress or setbacks throughout the European manufacturing group. Like a management andon, these systems would allow me—at a macro level—to regularly gather facts and data and stay abreast of our most impactful problems. At a micro level, they would surface problems that could prevent us from reaching our goal, which all management, staff, and employees would then explore and solve.

For example, we made our computer screens prompt us of real-time operational conditions at all of the European plant assembly lines. When we saw a problem, we could ask our staff if they had already responded to the problem. If not, we would call the manufacturing plant to find out more about the problem or enlist our staff to contact plants to take action. These new management systems enabled us to aggressively monitor our progress in resolving critical problems.

Inaccurate cost planning	**Unmotivated people**	**No risk management**
Sample vs. total gap	Poor treatment of Belgium	High destination mix impact
Plan vs. actual gap	No development system	High currency risk
Price and specification gap	Unable to hire talented people	Labor dispute risk
	No incentive for high performers	

Our eventual success in the European manufacturing group was mainly because we had broken down a huge problem into actionable items for all management—including Toyota Japan and the European Sales & Marketing group, which had largely been removed from overall profitability responsibility. Through annual hoshin deployment we showed members the direction—the vision—and the necessary conditions and activities that needed to take place. We constantly shared the progress of our problem-solving efforts and established new requirements that could drive us toward our common goals:

- Improve alignment of Toyota's European companies, including manufacturing operations in France, Poland, Turkey, and the UK; a joint venture with PSA in (then) Czechoslovakia; head office functions in Brussels for Manufacturing, Engineering, and Sales & Marketing; and distributors in 19 European country markets

- Improve revenue

- Capture cost reductions

- Motivate the workforce

- Optimize manufacturing companies and their assets and investments.

Actions that management and members took are applicable to any large management problems: Break down a large, vague problem into manageable pieces. Moving from one large problem to 28 more-manageable problems allowed us to distribute responsibilities for problem solving and to more accurately identify gaps and causes.

For example, inaccurate cost planning was broken down into a series of gaps. We gathered facts, analyzed data, and grasped the current conditions to clarify the degree of the problem. We discovered many hidden problems, such as cost planning for a new vehicle that was based on unrealistic assumptions, which in turn, led to huge losses after launch (i.e., a plan vs. actual gap). Manufacturing had overestimated plant capacity to reduce the fixed cost. Sales & Marketing had overestimated the new vehicle price for select major markets (UK, German, Italy). As a result, the planned price was higher than actual average price in the 19 markets in which the vehicles would be sold.

Ongoing losses had lead to people making unrealistic projections. In the planning stage, executives frequently made a new product profitability look better than what could be achieved. I was the one who had to point out that these wrong assumptions had become problems; clarify the real planned cost of the manufacturing based on current maximum capacity; and select a feasible price based on all 19 markets.

Most important, I got everyone to comprehend the problems associated with these practices. Japan and the US had been able to get away with such practices because plant capacity was rising with new investments—which Europe could not afford—and there was little price variation across their markets. European executives believed they could make similar assumptions. With the problem identified, for the first time we clearly knew how much we had to reduce cost and how much the sales price had to increase to be profitable. Responsibility, ownership, and a willingness to solve the problem could now begin.

Identify problems beyond our control and enlist support. Toyota's European Sales & Marketing group was mainly driven by volume or market share and was less concerned about profitability of operations at large. The profitability of Sales & Marketing had been secured by a positive, set margin between distribution prices to its sales arms and our ex-factory prices from manufacturing. Sales prices had been established for 19 country markets with approval of Toyota Japan. So a similar product had different prices in 19 different markets. In all but three European markets, manufacturing was losing money and every loss was realized by the manufacturing companies, not Sales & Marketing. Thus, the more we shipped to lower-price, money-losing markets, the more we suffered. And the sales volumes for these losing markets were increasing.

The Sales & Marketing group had also requested special price incentives (e.g., for the rental-car market). Such practices had been established when all vehicles were being imported from Japan, which helped to drive up market share in Europe. But the practices had not been reviewed in years, even after the start of production in the UK in 1991. These incentives could not be sustained by the UK manufacturing arm alone, and all capital was quickly depleted. Toyota had to inject capital into the UK manufacturing company twice in 10 years.

We asked European Sales & Marketing and Toyota Japan to stop such incentives and to set up a unified price scheme rather than 19 different prices, to enable us to establish a clear cost-reduction target. Otherwise we were subject to more and more cost-reduction requirements as low-priced sales volumes increased. We also requested Toyota Japan to establish a bonus scheme for all European executives, including those leading Sales & Marketing, that reflected overall European profitability.

Our hope was that this would eventually change their practices. To get their attention we sent reports to the European Sales & Marketing group and Toyota Japan that detailed how bad the profitability for manufacturing was in each of the money-losing markets. With a voluntary import restriction aimed at Japanese automakers in Europe, they could see how this was hurting their hope to localize more products for increased sales. Because now they could see problems clearly, the Sales & Marketing group agreed, with help from Toyota Japan, to step-by-step price unification across Europe, lowering of incentives, and a goal of European profitability.

In 2002, we presented our problem finding at an annual European meeting at which all top Toyota executives attended, including President Fujio Cho. He took this presentation as my problem finding report, which he had requested of me before I went to Europe. Our facts convinced all parties to change many bad practices.

Conduct benchmarking studies to identify major targets. I felt we needed to clarify how costs for our big-ticket items (those accounting for 60% to 70% of total cost) compared to what our competitors and other Toyota organizations in Japan and the United States were doing. We discovered that our wages were competitive (not too high), but that we needed to improve labor efficiency compared with Japan plants. We also found that costs associated with depreciation were extremely high due to heavy investments against small volumes and fewer operational hours. Other non-competitive costs included diesel engines and some purchased parts.

We confirmed these cost problems with facts, and staff at each of the manufacturing operations continued benchmarking studies in order to quantify the problems (identify the size of the gap). We shared this information with European Sales & Marketing and Toyota Japan at another Europe meeting and enlisted their help with issues under their control. Toyota Japan took responsibility to redesign the expensive diesel engine in order to be competitive. And our folks clearly understood how much we had to improve our side of the cost problem.

Unite an organization. I came to realize that our Brussels office had been acting as a service provider and coordination office for all the separate European manufacturing companies. This contrasted sharply with a leadership role, as had been spelled out in the original European plan. Evidently, the over-arching leadership role had not been communicated clearly. Executives at the individual European companies were reluctant to accept an additional leadership layer and President Toyoda's predecessor in Brussels had not been interested in fighting that battle. Thus, manufacturing companies acted independently.

It became clear that many of manufacturing's problems existed because the group lacked unity. We could not attack our problems as one organization if we did not think and act as one organization. To this end, President Shuhei Toyoda and I agreed to declare that the Europe Manufacturing head office would be based in Brussels, and the manufacturing companies in the UK, France, Turkey, and Poland would operate as a single entity under the direction of the Brussels office. Now, instead of a vague position as a support company for four independent companies, the Brussels office would become the European manufacturing headquarters.

Because I had a similar problem in the United States when designing and forming Toyota's North American manufacturing headquarters, we moved swiftly to incorporate the necessary structures in Europe. We clearly defined the authority between headquarters and each manufacturing company, as well as the reporting relationships. Even the capital relationship was revised, such as transferring Turkey plant stock owned by Toyota Japan to the Brussel head office.

In order to facilitate swift strategical deployment and cost reduction across the manufacturing group, we also consolidated functions such as financing, purchasing, logistics, production engineering, and information technology at the new Brussels headquarters, and pulled the R&D function out of the Sales & Marketing group. As part of this reorganization, all executives, including expats from Japan, were evaluated based on a unified appraisal system to promote the shared goals and values.

Establish common direction and alignment around an ideal state. The European manufacturing companies had nearly become independent, with only some direction from Toyota Japan. They regarded the establishment of the European headquarters as an infringement on their autonomy and a cost burden (they were charged a management fee). They were initially uncooperative. However, with a single structure in place we were able to develop a group vision and set a direction: "We aim to become an integrated and self-reliant operation, establishing a sustainable presence in Europe and securing profitable growth."

In 2002, Toyota Japan further clarified our direction by establishing a goal to make Europe profitable in 2005, with 1.2 million vehicle sales and €1 billion profit contributing to the Toyota 2010 vision. Along with these mid- and long-term directions, we established a Europe Manufacturing hoshin (a first) to realize our vision, and we aligned each manufacturing company hoshin with the Europe hoshin so that we could share challenges going forward.

With our group vision and hoshin deployment, we annually measured and confirmed individual performance activities and targets to assure that all European management and staff actions were focused on our hoshin objectives. We also reviewed these measures periodically as new problems surfaced—constantly reminding everyone of our ideal conditions and vision.

I reviewed my staff's hoshin progress every other week, and discussed my activity with our president and obtained his approval. My 2002 hoshin activity was straightforward but huge: integration of European manufacturing organizations, systems, and people, and developing a hoshin, KPIs, and common business practices for IT, production planning, logistics, accounting, financing, ex-factory pricing, corporate planning, and HR.

Establish systems to assess the organization's ability to find and solve problems. To get continuous-improvement underway, I first set up a monthly financial and cost analysis reporting system that compared current conditions against the budget for each European manufacturing company and the Brussels office. I used this to identify itemized cost-reduction problems and their impact on profitability.

I asked our staff to provide these reports each month as soon as they were available. They resisted at first, but eventually succumbed to my insistence and provided reports just eight working days after the monthly close, allowing us to quickly see and solve problems. Unlike previous reviews when only the total costs vs. total budget were assessed, we looked at a range of indicators that could surface problems:

- Itemized variable costs per actual unit against budget: Labor cost, for example, was followed by euro per product to encourage improving labor efficiency. Total labor against budget could be misleading when volume changed.

- We still looked at some higher-level financial results, such as profit by product and by a manufacturing company, with those groups responsible for each deviation. If a company raised profit due to favorable currency exchange, we discounted those results and focused on problems such as labor efficiency and material and energy usage, items for which the company was responsible.

- Uncontrollable external factors (e.g., sales volumes, price, model mix, and currency exchange rates) were reported to help clarify and understand their impact on our problems.

- Items for which the Brussels office was responsible— such as design, logistics, IT, administrative costs, and purchased parts—were analyzed to clarify who should tackle problems that emerged in these areas.

We also introduced unified accounting principles and a common IT system across the organizations in five countries. This facilitated quick reports, analysis, and common understanding. We shared these reports with the Sales & Marketing group to let them know what we were doing to encourage their sales price improvement.

Second, we introduced seven sets of KPIs to clarify actions needed to improve financial results and cost reductions:

- Production
- Quality
- Profit/Cost
- Safety
- Purchased parts
- People
- Environment

For example, for production KPIs, we started with the metrics of production plan vs. actual ratio, operation availability ratio, and labor hours per product. These KPIs were further broken down into drivers to enable responsible parties to take action on each function or job when they found underperforming KPIs. We presented all of the findings graphically in order to illuminate problems and drive quick actions.

Establish milestone meetings to communicate progress. We established multi-layer committees that manufacturing either led or participated in. These allowed all European executives to present and discuss difficult problems and collectively formulate countermeasures to address them:

- The Executive Committee inside our Brussel head office, worked on European manufacturing headquarters issues with participation by the headquarters officers, including presidents of manufacturing companies, major functional heads, myself, and President Toyoda.

- The Joint Executive Committee was a cross-company meeting with executives of the four manufacturing companies and the Brussels office executives.

- The European Executive Committee: executives from the Brussels offices, Toyota Japan, European manufacturing companies, and the Sales & Marketing group.

- The European Strategy Committee consisted of the top European executives and five senior managing directors, who were responsible for major functions in global Toyota.

These committees met regularly—weekly, monthly, quarterly depending on the group—to share and address problems. Without these meetings we would not have been able to consolidate common functions from the manufacturing companies into European headquarters in such a short period of time, nor could we have put pressure on European Sales & Marketing to allow increased ex-factory prices. More importantly, the meetings helped us to develop a leadership culture as one organization. In 2003, Toyota Motor Europe, presided over by Shuhei Toyoda, was established to facilitate collaboration among all parties in Europe. All of Toyota's European operations were now unified under this Toyota Motor Europe,

Because initially neither the individual manufacturing companies nor the Sales & Marketing group were cooperative with our Brussels head office, it was critical that we accurately articulated problems and shared all information available with others face-to-face. Everyone needed to see and recognize problems clearly and trust that they were seeing the real, true facts together. The KPI system and milestone meetings allowed us to share and discuss our discoveries and helped us achieve our common interest, supported by a common vision/hoshin.

Encourage team efforts and help others when they face problems beyond their capacity. Our Brussels head office staff was often not strong enough to break the resistance of the Sales & Marketing group or the manufacturing companies. This was not surprising; I had expected many difficulties as we tried to implement countermeasures upon finding problems. I had seen it four years earlier at the North American manufacturing head-quarters in Kentucky. I was determined to help our staff over-come such resistance, which they could not break on their own.

For example, the general manager of Accounting & Finance for the Brussels head office was blocked from attending UK cost meetings because the UK president insisted they should only discuss such issues internally. As previously discussed, people don't like to expose their problems to others. But I knew it was important for the UK to openly discuss their problems with us. So, I quickly began participating in those lower-level meetings as an "observer" (as a higher ranked officer from European head-quarters, I could not be refused participation). But I did more than observe in the meetings. I helped them to see their problems in a productive manner so that, in the future, we could avoid the unnecessary end-around behavior and openly discuss the UK problems.

Another example of the need for outside support was in trying to achieve process-time reductions for logistic routing planning (from six weeks down to two weeks) in order to reduce unplanned logistics costs. A six-week advanced routing plan could not accommodate changes that emerged from monthly production changes, and it usually led to unplanned logistic expenditures. Our biggest logistic losses were emergency shipments, often by air transportation rather than less costly ground transportation. Our staff could not solve this issue alone because they had been required to give each plant one full week just to check the logistics plan due to past errors in planning.

I stepped in and asked if the check was truly necessary. The answer was "No." I instructed staff to have the plant check the logistics plan while the plan proceeded (i.e., proceed unless halted). This approach was accepted by the plants and eventually the checking process was eliminated altogether, reducing the planning time. This, along with kaizen of logistics planning, enabled us to save several million euros.

Commend staff for their efforts when they find problems, solve problems, and make progress, and share good results. I love to find and solve problems, and I enjoyed helping staff find and work through problems. For example, it was fun to check our logistics scheduling board every day to see if staff had placed a blue dot (on time) or a red dot (behind schedule) on the board. The logistic department had been challenged to reduce planning time from six weeks to two weeks. They got it down to three weeks by working out many supplier problems, and they got it down to two weeks by implementing updated software. During this process, I regularly shook hands with the assistant manager when I saw a blue dot and asked about problems when a red dot appeared.

I also asked for a monthly cost-impact report from the logistics department to better understand how they were managing costs. They had improved the overall cost efficiency of logistics by reducing urgent airfreight shipments and special package arrangements. But, to my surprise, it took months for the actual savings to show up because of an accounting-payment delay as we waited on logistics billing. I asked accounting and logistics to work out a solution that would give more immediate insight into logistics costs trends, and they came up with a self-billing invoice system based on our accurate routing schedule; if our self-billing was incorrect, the supplier had to prove the error for payment to be corrected. This visibility allowed us to more rapidly see activities that were improving or hurting our logistics costs.

Logistics staff were engaged and excited to have the attention of a senior executive every day (I kid you not) and made progress step-by-step, seeing their savings monthly and discussing ways to improve the next month. They also felt the recognition and pride from their problem solving and, eventually, their accomplishments—the staff reduced annual logistic costs by nearly €30 million in two years.

Success from Finding and Solving Problems, Starts at the Top

As an organization, our problem-finding systems helped us to isolate and attack our problems, even though management and associates within the European manufacturing companies were initially weak at problem solving. Local management had trouble breaking down a problem such that their staff could be engaged and take action. They and their staffs also had trouble identifying root causes when a problem surfaced. To get this situation resolved as rapidly as possible, we forced them to learn problem solving quickly, starting with top executives. And the stakes for them were high—their promotion.

We asked candidates for executive positions to present problem-solving reports on their major business. If they did not report on a major problem or their report was not logical and sound, they were not promoted to the recommended position. For example, a candidate for a VP position in a manufacturing company presented his problem-solving report to me, President Toyoda, and the VP Human Resources; his company president attended in a supporting role for his candidacy. This was typical for reviewing promotions. More than half of the candidates failed, which, in turn, embarrassed their presidents who had recommended them. Soon candidates and presidents became very serious about teaching and learning problem solving.

Our practice for the promotion reviews improved problem-solving capabilities drastically. Of course, many high-ranking executives were furious, which merely drove them to improve the problem-solving capability in their companies, for executives as well as subordinates. (When we conducted problem-solving training in Georgetown, we focused first on lower-level members. After the European experience, I realized that the Georgetown approach took more time to instill a problem-solving culture due to insufficient encouragement from higher-level management.)

With this approach to people development and a detailed set of KPIs and a KPI tree in each company, we soon developed a systematic way to break down large problems, find root causes of the smaller problems, and establish goals and actions to address those root causes. Based on problem-solving methods rather than historical practices or gut beliefs, senior executives made large, fundamental changes to our business. This was a big departure from how Toyota European Manufacturing had operated.

For example, to address lack of revenues we strengthened our production flexibility to accommodate fluctuation of demand, which allowed us to share manufacture of one popular product in two different companies. This allowed us to accommodate increasing sales demand and improved production efficiency. We also increased local value-added content by establishing a parts business, including diesel engines and past-model service parts, and we soon started to export product to Japan and Mexico. We increased the capacity of our European plants without significant investment, including the addition of a third shift in France to meet higher demand (which also reduced our depreciation cost). For cost reductions, we set a number of objectives by all itemized costs—including purchased parts, depreciation, labor, material, energy, water, financial interest, administration, maintenance, logistics, warranty and so on. Each party responsible for these had to detail the actions they were taking, including introduction of investment controls.

Turning around the long-term losses in just three years certainly was regarded as impossible by those in Europe when I arrived. Yet when we broke down this big problem into smaller pieces and actionable items, it began to look tamer, albeit still challenging. We even successfully managed our currency risks, which had hurt our profitability, as they fluctuated and were thought to be beyond our control. We got Turkish suppliers to accept payment in euros (instead of lira) and customers in Poland to pay in euros (instead of zloty), resulting in us needing to manage only euros and yen. Exporting European made cars to Japan was also designed to reduce Japanese yen risk. We could use the yen from that export business to pay for the import parts from Japan, which neutralized currency risk.

We tirelessly broke down every detail of our problems, and prioritized our actions based on the impact that improvement would have on our big problem—lack of profit. Our systems monitored our actions and surfaced new problems as we moved toward our ultimate objective. By 2002, European operations losses were down to approximately €200 million. By 2003, we had a small profit. In 2004, we posted a profit of more than €300 million.

How Do I Know It's a Problem?

Do you approach each day looking for problems and improvement? Is your organization driven to relentlessly exhibit kaizen culture and problem-finding behaviors, with everyone in the company actively seeking to find problems and constantly searching for breakthroughs to achieve a shared vision? Do your management and workforce have the capacity to find and solve problems? Have you established systems that illuminate problems and motivate management and the workforce to address them? Losing hundreds of millions of dollars can fuel the drive to find problems, as we found out, but you should not have to be so unprofitable to take such actions.

Many companies do not have a common vision among senior management and lack an urgency for problem finding at the leadership level. (This certainly was the case in Europe.) We often find earnest problem finding within companies, but frequently done to address immediate, plant floor, or technical problems— often without a connection to a shared corporate vision. We also see organizations where little real problem finding occurs among leadership, management, or the workforce. All three instances make continuous improvement difficult if not impossible.

Many executives like to call a problem an "opportunity" because it removes the negative connotation of the word, problem. Phooey! Call a problem a "problem!" The word opportunity implies that you have some kind of choice in the matter as to whether you tackle it or not—a problem offers little choice but to solve it.

I have never seen a person who saw a
problem clearly and did nothing

— Fujio Cho

If a person sees a falling rock over their head, they must run away to avoid it. But if that person does not see the rock or the problem—thus not able to avoid it—they could die. Treat your problems like falling rocks. And just as important, you need the means to see them.

Toyota leadership developed systems that constantly forced problems to emerge (rocks to fall). They shared visions of created problems that few could have imagined without such a leadership push. Importantly, that push was accompanied by the means to develop solutions with a sense of urgency that addressed root causes of problems and collectively moved Toyota toward its shared vision. These systems surfaced problems that impacted daily improvements to meet performance expectations, as well as long-term improvements and innovative breakthroughs.

Toyota's manufacturing companies in Europe had strayed from this approach. I needed to reinforce the foundational role of senior leadership and re-establish (or possibly just establish) a kaizen culture. The Brussel office had been established in 2000, as a support office for Toyota's European manufacturing companies. The top executive was also chairman of the UK manufacturing company, and all other executives were Japanese and UK expats. All expats were expected to return to their original countries after a three- to five-year assignment. Lower-level employees were hired from Belgium or other European countries, principally for administrative jobs.

The original European leadership was not in favor of a true headquarters-like role, believing it would threaten the autonomy of the manufacturing companies and add an unnecessary layer of control. It was not surprising that UK expats and local employees were not motivated to accomplish critical tasks, let alone develop any kind of kaizen spirit. Japanese expats also wondered how to approach their relatively short-lived roles, and the French and UK companies viewed them as an extra administrative burden.

When new President Shuhei Toyoda and I got to Europe, we strongly felt it was necessary to establish our mission quickly to motivate the headquarters employees. Even before talking about kaizen culture, we took the initiative to clarify our role and responsibility, to describe the challenges ahead of us, and to express the concerns of Toyota Japan about the rising losses in Europe. Shuhei Toyoda, who also held the senior managing director position in Toyota Japan, was prudent to pursue a path to unify all the European organizations. He agreed that we should solidify our role as headquarters for Europe Manufacturing operations and that all manufacturing companies should work as a single entity. We clarified the authority and responsibility of each company and their reporting relationships, as well as graded and ranked all executive positions in Europe Manufacturing to prepare us to work together without turf battles.

The president of the French operation (who was Japanese) criticized the consolidation plan, but the president of the UK operation (who was British) was cooperative but apprehensive; he believed the Japanese network was typically off limits and decisions were made behind the scenes without local input.

Now with roles, responsibilities, reporting relationships, and decision-making mechanisms defined and clearer to European executives, he and a few others were ready to change. The local executives began to respect the Brussels office as European head-quarters, although we still needed to prove and improve our capabilities to lead others. For example, we would be in charge of Europe Manufacturing profitability, but we really had no way to see profitability in a timeframe that allowed us to affect it.

Initially three organizations would be consolidated into the financial statement—the Brussels head office, UK (an assembly plant and an engine plant), and France (one startup assembly plant). Because the head office had been an administrative service organization and received a management fee from the manufacturing companies, they historically had disclosed only to Toyota

Japan. We could not see timely profit or loss conditions clearly and could not obtain the cost of Japan parts: we received two-month old financial results from Japan, we had no cost-planning expert in Europe to break down overall product cost into detail, and we did not have a system or the responsibility to gather the necessary information and regularly analyze data. We quickly demanded the transfer of financial responsibility and the addition of an on-staff cost planning expert, and we installed the same computer system used by the European Sales & Marketing group, which allowed us to swiftly communicate and transfer accounting information in Europe.

You should be able to recognize components of your story and pursuit of kaizen in our European story. Developing a kaizen culture needs to start with a rigorous pursuit of *fact finding*:

- What value does your organization deliver?

- What is its mission?

- How should your company go about its business?

- What products or services will you provide?

- Who are your customers, and what do they want?

- What related organizations, internally or externally, will you look to for support in pursuing your mission?

- How good or bad is your situation?

- What is your big (or small) problem?

- Who is responsible for specific tasks in the organization and for finding problems and improving these conditions?

- How capable is upper management and the workforce to take on these tasks?

These are all big questions that typically only senior leaderships can begin to answer—and the answers and subsequent actions must be based on facts. In Europe, a lot of people had not paid attention to the European losses and simply did what they were told. Or if they paid attention, they regarded the huge loss as beyond their responsibility. Facts would wake them up and help to decide next steps.

We used the questions above to assess our current conditions and to identify breaking points of the problem. We did this to establish some basic stability before starting into strategic planning/hoshin management and execution. We met with our leadership staff and asked them the questions. Could they clarify the mission, describe their understanding the mission, and identify their roles and responsibilities in supporting the mission?

When all the facts were presented and we were confident that management clearly understood our mission and our real status, only then did we begin hoshin management. Hoshin management sets a path for where your organization should go (should-be conditions) and the actions and time it will take to get there. "What" is identified as the gap between should-be conditions and current conditions. In Europe, the gap was €1.1 billion (current loss €500 million plus the future target of €600 million profit). The time when you begin hoshin management may be the first time that you and your staff really see the full picture of your organization and the enormity of the challenges ahead.

At the Brussels office, we had to collect a lot of customer information to detail should-be conditions, including profitability. We established and monitored key performance indicators (KPIs) for the entire manufacturing operation, including indicators to gauge headquarters' efficiency on our direct contributions, such as office headcount ratio, purchasing cost reduction, and investment cost reduction. We used TQM principles to objectively assess our current conditions, and then started discussions about the manufacturing group hoshin with the individual manufacturing company executives. We reviewed hoshin-planning frameworks, like business environment, which helped to improve alignment among the companies and with the head office.

It took a full day just to discuss hoshin planning, but it was an important time for all of us to clarify our own mission. We also welcomed manufacturing company presidents as officers in the new Brussels office, which would improve their ownership of the group hoshin and attention to the common KPIs.

With a hoshin-management system and KPI structure, we were able to apply measures and tools that brightly illuminated myriad problems that contributed to our profitability problem. Once a problem was seen—a falling rock identified—and people understood their mission, they started looking for solutions. This was the start of a kaizen culture in Europe.

Any change in behavior for an individual or an organization must be nurtured, monitored, and informed by feedback. Systems will allow you to do that. They provide a framework to change behaviors and develop kaizen culture, establishing the habits of problem finding and problem solving among senior leadership, management, and the workforce. This is what eventually happened in Europe. We changed from a disjointed organization that lacked the will or means for real problem solving to one tightly aligned to our hoshin. The two Toyota systems of hoshin management and KPIs, and the means to manage them, helped us to address our multimillion-dollar problem.

Plan and Share the Vision

It is the responsibility of *leadership to lead* others in finding and solving problems in an organization. This was true in Europe and it began with a vision. Initially, the vision was "Three-year turn around," and was later elaborated to, "We aim to become an integrated and self-reliant operation, establishing a sustainable presence in Europe and securing profitable growth." Everyone in the company understood the vision and it starkly contrasted current conditions—a minor, unprofitable competitor in Europe made up of independent Engineering, Manufacturing, Sales & Marketing, and Distribution companies, each of which required financial, material, and technical support from Toyota Japan.

The huge contrast and gap between our current condition and the vision depressed most people at first. But, we knew it was possible to inspire others to find and solve problems once the huge problem was broken down into manageable pieces. We could, as the saying goes, eat the elephant one bite at a time.

This simple but challenging concept of identifying the big problem and a vision for improvement, and then breaking the problem into manageable pieces is an opportunity for leaders and management teams to both lead organizations to success and motivate their workforces. But it requires some guts.

Many executives refrain from presenting a vision that could be perceived as absurd rather than achievable. They fear negative external reactions (business analysts, financial markets) to big ideas or internal demoralization ("We can never achieve that!"). Or they are just too comfortable with the status quo and unwilling to present a challenge and take on the work to achieve it. None of these conditions will inspire your members for kaizen.

Your shared vision should be a long-term, never-ending mission—it *should* create discomfort, even ridicule. To make a long-term vision truly shareable, it must offer leadership, management, and the workforce a means to *incrementally* act on it.

Hoshin management is the process to share and break down your vision. Many executives believe that their company practices something similar to hoshin management—"strategy deployment" or "policy deployment" or traditional "management by objectives". But what we see across industry is really dramatically different from Toyota-style hoshin management:

- Old-fashioned strategic planning, where a plan is created but *seldom shared* beyond senior executives.

- A plan is shared throughout the company but functions and management *fail to identify their mission and roles* and see no way to help the company achieve the plan.

- A plan is shared in which targets are narrowly defined financial metrics for reporting purposes, and once they have been reported, the process starts again, without specific actions to improve gaps that existed—*no PDCA*.

The first step in establishing hoshin management is organizational *condition* improvement for long-term success. It is not based on financial targets, but objectives that will improve your organization's condition, allow it to consistently produce expected results, and progressively move it toward the vision.

Think in terms of *condition* management rather than *target* management. Hoshin management asks the question, "What kind of condition do we want to create?" This question opens up all kinds of opportunities for improvement. Everyone can participate in the condition and translate it personally to their work, and in doing so decide their own best way to contribute.

Hoshin management poses a condition first and only then applies a numerical target as a key indicator or major activity to be accomplished. A good hoshin condition could be "Develop a strong organization that is able to reduce costs constantly and beat competitor pricing." Given such a should-be condition, even a safety specialist might consider how a safer workplace contributes to cost reductions (e.g., reducing work-related injuries lowers insurance costs, improves morale, boosts productivity).

The advantage of condition management is that management *does not have to point out where the problems are* in an entire organization to achieve the should-be condition. Individuals within the organization will figure out where the problems are and communicate this, along with their improvement activities and the goals of those activities (i.e., goal-setting occurs in conjunction with senior leadership, not because senior leadership dictated it). And because individuals have a role in defining their workplace, their activities, and their goals, their behaviors begin to change.

If management within our European operations had to detail our strategy specific to every member at the Brussels head office and for those within the manufacturing companies, we would still be working on the challenge. Instead, every member was requested to propose activities to solve their own problems in through catchball with their supervisor. This practice automatically enabled us to develop a comprehensive, detailed strategy map and follow our progress.

As a second step in hoshin planning, you need supporting, timed levels of hoshin management. Just as a problem is broken down, so are hoshin milestones:

- *Midterm hoshin*: This includes directional condition and a prioritization of major activities for the next three to five years. The midterm hoshin is reviewed and modified gradually every year to accommodate changes in the business environment, as well as failures and successes of the previous year's activities, the results of which are seen through an annual hoshin progress check. The midterm hoshin is reestablished in its entirety every three to five years to further challenge the organization. For example, a midterm hoshin for a vision of "Develop a strong organization that is able to reduce costs constantly and beat competitor pricing," could be "Implement lean system effectively throughout organization."

- *Annual hoshin:* This includes more specific hoshin activities and associated targets that move an organization toward the conditions established in the midterm plan. Targets are usually concrete activities with timing established and KPIs to measure the target. (KPIs may occasionally be targets.) KPIs measure overall performance and can be monitored to check most daily activities and develop the capability to understand the daily workings of the organization. From a midterm hoshin "Implement a lean system effectively throughout organization," an annual hoshin could be "Standardize all production processes and introduce kanban by the end of the year." The target could be "100% standardization of production processes and kanban in place by December."

Mr. Ohno (elimination of waste) and Mr. Okuda (environmental leader) offered unrealistic visions that spurred innovation of an improvement system (the Toyota Production System) and an energy-efficient vehicle (Prius). Neither could be achieved overnight; they required a disciplined system by which Toyota translated their long-term vision into more tangible three-to-five year visions with annual short-term objectives.

In Europe and the United States, we repeatedly found varied and contrasting understandings of hoshin among staff, including expats from Japan. We needed to get back to the basics. Hoshin management had been used in Toyota since 1961, but it began to look more like a management task list or as a means to secure resources. It also was communicated only to Japanese expats—not to Western management in English. Not surprisingly, hoshin management in Toyota had lost its effectiveness.

The globalization of Toyota in the 1990s was an opportunity to take hoshin management back to its origins. I requested that our TQM division compile official hoshin guidance—in English—to use outside of Toyota. Because this guidance had not been in place, each individual had implemented their own interpretation of hoshin management, particularly outside Japan. We used the guidance document developed by our TQM division to teach hoshin management in the United States and Europe (see *Hoshin Management System* at right).

Hoshin Management System

A hoshin statement should clearly show all individuals your organization's gaps between the target condition and the current condition. And it must provide everyone with room for their own interpretation of the statement to apply to their specific responsibility and the means to establish measurements by which to gauge progress—a major activity to be accomplished within a specific timeframe or occasionally a key performance indicator (KPI) to gauge success or failure.

Top management initiates the hoshin, which is cascaded down through management and individual team members so they can develop their own themes to support the hoshin. (The Europe Manufacturing group hoshin was equivalent to a division hoshin in the diagram below.)

Hoshin management is not one directional. It also is a top-down and bottom-up process, with catchball between levels to decide an individual's annual hoshin and priorities as part of performance management.

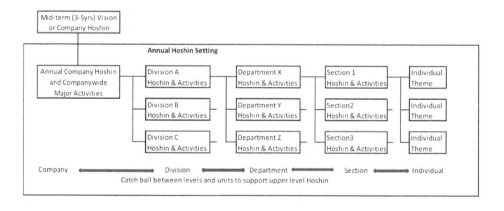

For the Europe Manufacturing group, we developed a hoshin that was coordinated with the Toyota headquarters hoshin and the group's 2010 vision. (See Appendices: *TMEM Hoshin for 2004*). It included our vision statement, major activities to be accomplished within a timeframe, activity leaders, and the main and affiliated departments to proceed with the hoshin. This high-level hoshin required clear leadership, detailed roles and responsibilities, and collaboration among divisions or departments.

Cooperation among responsible parties was critical for every group-wide hoshin. Not surprisingly, the hoshin related to the consolidation of manufacturing functions created resistance from parties that were losing a function. For example, we tried to consolidate the purchasing function of the Turkey plant into the Brussels office where former UK purchasing took care of French plant needs. Turkey could not resist officially because of efficiency improvements and cost reductions, but they complained to Toyota Japan and questioned our capabilities. As a result, implementation of hoshin in these areas was delayed. Eventually, constant dialogue with the Turkey Manufacturing president, regular visits to Turkey, and a technical compromise reduced resistance. Turkey purchasing executives gradually welcomed the opportunity to work with the European operation where more promotion opportunities would be available to them.

A few hoshin objectives, such as consolidation of all Europe's IT functions had to be revised. Because of resistance, we had to settle on co-locating IT staff at both Manufacturing and Sales & Marketing locations, but we were able to establish one common data center. The lesson: even high-level communications between senior leaders requires catchball.

While not perfect, our hoshin translated strategic intent of our European operations into an aligned, measurable, day-to-day business system, one that individual staff could independently act upon and improve. Each manufacturing company also developed its own hoshin to support the group hoshin targets as well as their own needs. Likewise, lower-level hoshin, such as department hoshin, were developed until hoshin reached individual activities.

Hoshin management drove us to check both the process and the results to see successes and failures—this allowed members to act to sustain a success or improve upon a failure in the next hoshin cycle. Remember that hoshin is "plan" and the annual activity is "do" of the PDCA cycle. We "checked" results against the hoshin, and then we "acted" to standardize good processes to sustain good results and continued to work on bad processes to get better results in the following year.

> Good KPIs are not something to meet or comply with—they establish measurable gaps used to develop actionable countermeasures.

Connecting Hoshin to Results and Problems

KPIs and other targets enable leadership and managers to see if activities are producing expected or desired results, including good performance of daily work or of work that over a longer term supports the target condition of a hoshin statement. Today, most companies track KPIs, but these are often part of an organizational scorecard and driven by financial statements. They tend to surface problems *after* the opportunity to correct them. Good KPIs are not something to "meet" or to comply with—they establish measurable gaps used to develop actionable countermeasures. They help break down a problem to secondary or lower indicators so that change can take place *before* outcomes are final. These secondary and lower indicators are often called "drivers" because they enable members to react to poor performance quickly.

Toyota's Single KPI

Toyota Japan used a single manufacturing KPI: productivity. Other factors—such as quality, safety, and employee morale—were determined to be drivers that boosted labor productivity. Because of the highly developed kaizen culture in Toyota Japan, management and employees intuitively made the connection between productivity, quality, safety, etc. They knew that good quality eliminates repair time and good safety eliminates lost time, both of which improve labor productivity. Safety, quality, and employee morale were separately monitored by divisions to ensure improvements occurred and that they were not compromised for the sake of productivity.

To ensure the connections to quality existed, productivity was calculated based only on good quality products. Cost was separately controlled, but its major focus was still productivity because, other than purchased parts, labor cost represents the most controllable cost in an assembly industry. (If you are an executive in a material industry, such as aluminum production, you might consider a KPI for yield ratio or energy consumption instead of productivity.)

On a monthly basis, we discussed productivity improvement toward the annual target at executive meetings at a host plant (rotated every month). At this meeting, we would check progress on site and share good kaizen cases of the host with others. Plant management checked progress on labor productivity and its drivers, such as quality, safety, run ratio of assembly, or daily equipment uptime based on a daily plant productivity indicator. Supervisors and group leaders calculated their own productivity *every day*, and they also tracked secondary indicators, such as hourly output with downtime minutes (as indicated with an on-site hourly output board), which forced them to rapidly fix problems that could erode productivity.

This system put tremendous pressure on Toyota Japan managers throughout their careers, and the workforce constantly felt this pressure as well. (All employees below the level of manager, including non-plant members, were paid a productivity allowance based on monthly manufacturing productivity.) Management reinforcement and the monetary incentive made productivity the single focused factor for all team members. They constantly tried to find and solve problems that hurt productivity: Engineers were keen to design easy-to-assemble products and easy-to-maintain equipment. Administration helped manufacturing stay focused on production. Schedulers worked to ensure level production and avoid work fluctuations that might require additional manpower.

This single KPI at Toyota Japan spurred amazing results: productivity increased 3–5% every year for almost a *half century*, even during times of recession or when Toyota was relinquishing production volume to overseas plants. Productivity improvement was perfectly matched to the elimination of all waste—Toyota's never-ending mission. Toyota used the highest productivity record to date for each process as the target for a new car model. Every new model was subject to a higher target, as it should be since it was produced with the most advanced equipment, tools, devices, and engineering and manufacturing methodology available to date. Thus, the productivity target consistently rose.

Toyota Japan established the means to surface problems (focus on an always higher productivity) and team members had a tool by which to specifically identify problems that prevented productivity improvement. Instead of asking members to simply find waste, the KPI motivated everyone to see a problem, such as downtime, and immediately relate it to productivity and Toyota's shared vision. Productivity improvement was seen as kaizen and a shared vision by all members, and it was recognized as a means to job security and better wages. The company benefitted and its members benefitted while working toward the shared should-be condition—mutual trust.

Why You Can't Use a Single KPI

For manufacturing operations outside of Japan, we knew we *could not* use a single productivity KPI for many reasons. First, a single KPI is unlikely to work with an organization that is just beginning to establish a kaizen culture. At both Toyota's North America and Europe Manufacturing operations, the relationship between productivity and other drivers (quality, safety, scheduling, conveyance efficiency, supplier performance, engineering) was not clearly understood and connected by management and members.

Second, lacking that connection and understanding, management and members would be unable to find the necessary range of problems; they would myopically focus on productivity. In fact, many Japanese managers who had relocated to North America and Europe objected to the idea of having the productivity pressure applied to them outside of Japan. They were fearful that local plant managers would focus on non-stop operations to hit the productivity KPI and ignore safety and quality (e.g., running the line even when problems emerged).

Instead, in both the United States and Europe, we adopted a set of KPIs that consisted of quality, safety, and morale. It was a challenging process. Despite the connection of these areas to productivity—as witnessed by Toyota Japan—these three KPIs could not sufficiently boost awareness of productivity problems to a level necessary for major cost kaizen. Our approach was backward: good quality, safety, and morale do not necessarily improve productivity, although good productivity needs good quality, safety, and morale.

In Georgetown, we first emphasized quality in order to compete with Camry benchmarks based on imports from Japan; we achieved our quality target early on and won J.D. Power awards. This did strengthen member morale, and more than 90% of employees said, "Georgetown was a good place to work." But the Georgetown safety record was mediocre due to many hand injuries, although still better than the industry average.

Continental's One KPI

Continental Airlines (since merged with United Airlines) adopted one, sole KPI in 1995: on-time schedule ratio. The KPI was accompanied by incentive pay in order to improve customer satisfaction. Continental had identified customer satisfaction as its shared vision and believed the measure could save the near-bankrupt organization. The following year, Continental received the J.D. Power award and avoided bankruptcy: all team members had easily focused on the single KPI of on-time schedule ratio and found problems that negatively impacted it. Employees focused on quick and accurate baggage handling, smooth seat assignment, proper equipment maintenance, better flight scheduling, fast customer-complaint settlement, etc., as the drivers to improve the KPI. Each individual was motivated (incentive pay) to find problems, and had a tool (KPI and drivers) by which to measure their own activities and identify a problem that could cause them to miss a flight schedule.[3]

The Georgetown incentive scheme was based on quality, safety, and attendance, while the one at the mother plant in Japan had been based on productivity. People in Georgetown tended to overly focus on quality and became nitpickers, so much so that the quality department had to provide boundary samples in order to reduce the identification of defects that were not really defects. Elimination of unnecessary work and productivity was important for managers, but not their primary objective. There also was little pressure on members to improve productivity, and, in fact, high overtime became a monetary incentive for certain people in order to support a high standard of living.

We should have put in place productivity measures against a standard at an early stage of operation. As the result, we had to introduce a productivity KPI in 2000, along with a broader set of

3. Gordon Bethune, *From Worst to First*, Wiley, 1999

KPIs. The set included nine categories and 16 individual KPIs. The 16 KPIs which were selected from *250 candidates* proposed by each function. 16 was better than 250, but still far too many to consider on a regular basis. We lacked the focus and effectiveness of the single KPI in Toyota Japan. However, a bonus for salaried team members was linked to the KPI results to promote value sharing among separate operations. So from that perspective, we felt that we were nurturing the growth of a kaizen culture, despite also knowing that we needed to whittle down our list of KPIs

Toyota Motor Manufacturing North America—Set of KPI

KPI category	Indicator
Total output	1. Revenue
	2. Volume
Cost	3. Cost reduction dollar
Profit	4. Operating profit margin
Productivity	5. Productivity index
	6. Administration staff ratio
Employee morale	7. Salaried turnover ratio
	8. Hourly attendance ratio
Safety	9. Lost time accident case
Quality	10. Defect per unit
	11. First-run ratio
	12. J.D. Power Initial Quality Survey
Production preparation for new model	13. Project ramp-up time
	14. Project implementation cost
Supplier performance	15. Supplier quality ratio
	16. On-time delivery ratio

(which we eventually did). We also realized that when function or department leaders are asked to develop KPIs, they invariably propose many of their own metrics as a way to get recognized. This quickly leads to a list of uncontrollable KPIs. Some proposed KPIs that were rejected:

- *Warranty claims*: Although a meaningful measure, it had too much of a time lag—six months, one year, three years—for us to react to current operations.

- *Head count*: Head count alone does not mean much because it can be driven upward by increasing production volume or the number of projects underway.

- *Capital investment*: Investment may or may not be effective, and needs to be evaluated in the context of overall cost reductions.

- *Litigation number*: This measure could be effective to improve CSR (corporate social responsibility), but it was too narrow of a scope of interest for ordinary members.

As you establish KPI, select a few that support your shared vision, e.g., *sales* for a customer-service oriented company; *profit* for shareholder-oriented company; *productivity* for a kaizen-oriented company; *safety* for a risk-associated company. Then have senior management break down those few KPIs to lower-level indicators or drivers. Each level then controls its own drivers and finds and corrects problems quickly that connect to the KPIs. Remember, the top-level KPIs you choose can be extended to people, organization, business knowledge, profit, etc., through secondary KPIs and drivers.

I encouraged this approach with both North America and Europe. Neither region reduced the number of KPIs drastically, but over time they each developed a KPI tree (see page 94) that established a good cause-and-effect relationship for each KPI, graphically presented so that they could see conditions at a glance.

KPI Tree

KPIs are effective for tracking performance and identifying problem areas, but they usually don't reveal the problems to attack. For example, when productivity has deteriorated, what is the specific problem? A KPI tree composed of second-, third-, fourth- and further-tier KPI drivers establishes cause-and-effect relationships.

For example, a productivity index, such as ratio of actual hours/standard hours, should be monitored as a first-tier KPI, with second-tiers of downtime ratio, repair time, etc. The second tier is driven by a third, such as downtime linked to machine downtime, work delay, material shortage, etc. Once this tree is developed and each index is monitored, management will pinpoint a problem area with the first-tier KPI, and then quickly go after a root cause through the tiers to improve the KPI.

To develop an effective KPI tree, develop a standard for each index so as to easily identify a problem: i.e., a deviation from standard. A target should be established based on what your organization needs to be competitive. The target you select should appear to be unachievable.

For example, when you benchmark competitors you may find that your operation is using twice the volume of labor when compared to competitors' operations. You should establish the target to the level of the competitors, setting labor at half that of your current operation. Closing the gap won't happen overnight, but doing this spurs every problem-solving effort to move the operation to the competitive level through step-by-step gap reduction. Display these indices on site to make problems visible to facilitate quick action for immediate solution.

For example in 2005, our UK operation developed a KPI tree for seven categories: quality, safety, volume, environment, people development, CSR, and cost/ROA. Every morning, management gathered and analyzed data on the seven and visually shared and responded to problems as a management team.

A single KPI is powerful and easier to focus on, but a well-organized set of KPIs and a KPI tree can be also be effective for seeing actionable problems quickly. Whether using a single good KPI or a good set of KPIs and a KPI tree, you should translate your vision into comprehensible terms. Remember these four keys when developing your KPI:

1. Keep them simple and well connected to the core vision of the organization to promote continuous improvement.

2. Have a standard against which to judge the current condition, and review it periodically to keep it competitive.

3. Use a KPI tree to break a KPI down into drivers or indices to find the real problem. Once management develops this tier system, you can monitor the first-tier KPI and then check the drivers when the first-tier KPI deteriorates.

4. Present KPIs visually with graphics and prominently display them so that conditions and trends can easily be seen before there is a critical breakdown in performance.

How Is Hoshin Working Out?

With hoshin and KPIs in place, how do you know that hoshin management is working and that all levels of the organization and all employees, top management to shopfloor, are acting on the shared vision in the long-term interest of customers (internal and external) and the enterprise? We used a system to identify gaps in the deployment of hoshin—which, ultimately, reveals gaps between customer satisfaction and the daily actions of management and the workforce.

We looked for:

- Breakdowns of business or information flow

- Lack of cooperation or sectionalism

- Inadequate leadership and strategy

- Lack of understanding of the hoshin and what's required (e.g., shared value, departmental mission, people development, work processes, information sharing, and target setting).

Our system for finding problems with hoshin management was called Management-quality Advancement System (MAST). Instituted in 2000, this self-assessment system was based on TQM concepts and consisted of baseline levels for each department's mission, vision, role, and responsibility (products and services to their customers and competitiveness of these offerings). Each baseline helps a department better understand the customers that receive their products and services (including internal customers) and the customers' satisfaction with the products and services. An awareness of internal customers is important because it encourages cooperation among departments and keeps them focused on the company hoshin (rather than only achievements of the department).

As a prerequisite for any hoshin deployment, we would gauge how clearly department management defined workplace baselines for the following eight elements:

- Business environment and anticipated changes

- Workplace role, mission, and vision

- Department hoshin in conjunction with higher hoshins (e.g., company hoshin)

- Products and services to be delivered

- Customers and their needs

- Related organizations in and outside company
- Key factors of success
- Benchmarks and KPIs to evaluate own competitiveness

These baselines drove the hoshin-assessment process and were clarified by the top of the organization. For example, hoshin development in Europe was managed by the Brussels office. At off-site regional meetings, we reviewed our baselines in relation to business environment changes, performance progress, problems with KPIs, current hoshin progress, the sales plan, upcoming major projects, and hoshin proposals for the coming year for Toyota Japan and for global Manufacturing.

We then discussed key factors for success in the coming year (e.g., major model changes, cross-functional cost improvements, etc.) and should-be or target conditions to be incorporated into the new hoshin proposal. We also reflected on past failures and higher-level baselines. The hoshin proposals would be modified through catchball between various levels.

Corporate planning drafted a European hoshin for regional top approval. The draft was confirmed among local executives and sent back to Toyota Japan for final review and catchball. Once the regional hoshin was established, it was announced and then each regional manufacturing and functional top executive proceeded to develop their own hoshin. These were then cascaded down to individual performance themes through catchball at each stage of the process. In the regional meetings, we also helped executives understand all hoshin elements and helped them develop their respective company and division hoshin in line with our baseline. The process worked like this in North America as well as Europe.

Toyota Japan defined its hoshin-assessment elements in elaborate detail. (See Appendices: *Hoshin-Assessment Elements for Toyota's Europe Manufacturing Group*). This level of detail was expected within Toyota, but it is not necessary for you to get started; you can add detail and supporting elements as you grow confident with your assessment system. The assessment elements at Europe Manufacturing helped us identify organizational problems and clarify our hoshin across European units and departments within the company, check smooth work flow and connection of the departments, and improve hoshin management and customer satisfaction.

Getting Started with a Hoshin-Assessment System

To get started with your own hoshin-assessment system, first identify ideal conditions for the key elements for your organization, and evaluate the current condition against an ideal condition. You can use the Toyota elements as your baseline, tailor elements to your company, or work from TQM principles.

Second, ask department heads to describe what currently is going on related to each element (departmental baseline) and to evaluate their department for each of the key elements. You will be surprised at the disconnection between your perspective of department capabilities and the perspectives of the department heads. Theoretically, if hoshin management is flawless, there is no variation in descriptions or in the scoring applied from department to department.

Regularly review your key elements with departments (at least annually), find problems in hoshin management within departments, and encourage the departments to identify the root causes of their hoshin-management problems and apply solutions to improve their baselines and, thus, improve a department capability to support the corporate long-term, mid-term, and annual hoshin.

Surface and Solve Major Manufacturing Problems

In our lead roles in Europe and elsewhere, we deployed two critical systems that had a profound impact: One system was focused on production efficiency (called "PEFF") and allowed top executives of the Europe Manufacturing companies to daily monitor and improve productivity and move us toward our profit objectives. A second system was used in our more advanced lean operations and focused on ROA (return on assets, calibrated by dividing operating profit by total assets). The ROA system was used to monitor and improve the use of assets and connect plant activities more closely to profitability.

Production Efficiency Connected to Profitability

In 2002, there were 570 employees in the Brussels head office and another 8,800 employees in our five European plants. This number grew rapidly as we expanded. There were countless operational problems every day that could arise and affect our ability to address our big problem (profitability). As a management team, we needed to see these issues *as they occurred* so that they did not snowball and make our big problem even bigger.

When President Toyoda and I arrived in Europe, operations could not meet any basic Toyota standards, such as 95% operation run ratio (uptime making good product as demanded). Although mother plants in Japan sent many expats to help, the European companies struggled, endured criticism, and lost confidence. One UK executive told me that the focus on cost reductions in every category (such as maintenance) actually led to increased equipment breakdowns, lower run ratios, more criticism, and no recognition of their cost reductions that were successful. A vicious cycle was underway.

We needed to develop strong management, systems, and member involvement capable of improving all aspects of operations in a manufacturing company—quality, safety, morale, productivity, maintenance, process engineering, production scheduling, parts delivery, etc. At the manufacturing head office we understood the drivers for the efficiency improvements of all these activities, but we could not monitor them from Brussels simultaneously. We could monitor first-tier KPIs, but we needed responsible people at each European site to monitor drivers, see problems quickly, and identify and fix root causes. The one KPI that provided an easy, effective link between the Brussels office and the Manufacturing companies was productivity.

Since the 1950s, Toyota had calculated a simple production efficiency percentage to track productivity:

Standard production time (*benchmark time for a product x the number of good quality products produced*)

Actual production time (*89% of paid working time*)

In 1995 this became an official measure of Toyota around the globe. The denominator accounts for 11% of non-production time or incidental work (e.g., breaks, on-site training, safety checks, quality circles, and kaizen activities) to ensure people development. We also assumed a fixed maintenance ratio—the more we improve direct labor productivity, the more maintenance performance needed to improve. (It should be a fixed percentage of direct labor hours, otherwise indirect labor could offset direct-labor reductions, such as the application of more automation.)

Labor productivity was measured at each production unit, which allowed us to aggregate it to represent a shop, department, or plant (even an entire company). Because production efficiency can be calculated daily or for longer periods, it surfaces labor productivity or operational problems in almost real time and forces kaizen. In labor-intensive environments such as the auto industry, production efficiency was especially effective for holding management accountable for labor costs.

With this production efficiency measure we were able to pinpoint a problem area and ask the responsible party to analyze major drivers, such as frequent line stops, poor quality, untimely parts delivery, injury, equipment breakdowns, inadequate training. But more importantly, it revealed trends in our manufacturing operations and allowed management to develop improvement targets associated with real labor-cost problems. Reported monthly in Europe, production efficiency provided a means to:

- Foster continuous kaizen activities

- Motivate all employees in cost-reduction activities

- Control hiring activities and resource acquisition (improvement meant less direct labor)

- Create a good understanding of shop, department, or plant conditions

- Provide upper management a *directional* gauge to the overall efficiency of the organization.

ROA Connected to Profitability

Prior to my time in Europe, we used ROA as a monthly key performance indicator at the Tsutsumi plant in Japan to identify problems with asset management and gain additional insights into productivity and profitability. This concept was not introduced within Europe Manufacturing until operations had become more mature. However, organizations with more fully implemented lean systems and making consistently good results need more sophisticated tools to find problems that can impact productivity and profitability.

ROA is helpful where senior executives have reservations about emphasizing an *operational* KPI, such as productivity. They argue that leadership is measured by and pressured to improve *financial* results, and that factors beyond productivity—such as

Getting Started with a Production Efficiency System

To introduce a production-efficiency system as we did in Europe, establish a benchmark time for the products or parts to be produced under each manager—they will be responsible for tracking production efficiency and improving the process. The benchmark time can be established by using one of the following measures or averaging the following measures:

- Results of motion studies done by engineering staff

- Target times for the products created by product-design engineers to establish product costs

- Process data developed by process engineers when designing the process.

Check your benchmark time with the target labor cost in the cost plan for a particular product to set a competitive labor-cost condition. The gap between current conditions and the benchmark time is the problem: it could stem from the design side or the current manufacturing environment or both. When you become aware of this gap, you will search for root causes in order to solve it. Eventually you will establish rules on how to decide on a more realistic benchmark time, and modify the rules and your system to accommodate the situations of all areas involved.

With a benchmark time established, collect production output for the shift by manager and his line supervisors. They should be able to tabulate good quality products or parts produced for their shift every day, ideally every hour on site to detect real time problems. Calculate standard production time for the shift or hour using the benchmark time and this output. Managers can use total working hours from daily payroll input data as the actual production time denominator. Note that a manager might be able to push production efficiency upward by reducing the percentage of incidental work (such as quality-control circles, on-site training for people development), but long-term the absence of incidental work will negatively affect productivity).

good products, assets, material, energy, engineering or sales costs—drive profit. I believe that when processes or operations are improved, a good business result will follow. But business management also requires forecasting and making decisions based on unforeseen events: What will demand be? How much should we invest? How much cash should we have? Management is measured by results that their decisions influence, and so management should be responsible for their forecasts (good or bad).

As tracking activities become stable, support them with a computer application or spreadsheets so that a manager can input more detail—such as working hours for repair time, waiting time, and out-of-control line stops. Information technology makes it easier to calculate a more defined percentage, but start first with a simple approach, and then apply IT, otherwise you run the risk of IT defining the process rather than management.

Start your production-efficiency tracking with a labor-intensive operation, such as assembly or welding, and for direct operators—these are the easiest to establish. Once you get experience, add other operations and indirect staff, such as maintenance, to control the labor costs of those personnel. Because the system is not 100% scientific— due to the manner of setting the benchmark time—focus on improvement trends, such as monthly or year-on-year improvements. Managers are more likely to accept your productivity system as a problem-finding tool if you focus on change rather than absolute figures: they will resist standalone results to evaluate labor performance, claiming inaccuracy of the established benchmark time or variability of process conditions.

We faced these questions both at the Tsutsumi plant in Japan and the Global Production Planning Division in Toyota City. We needed a system that could be used to not just understand the current situation of an operation, but relate the operation to overall company profitability. Our productivity measure worked, but we were concerned that plant management only focused on operational improvements (labor, material and utility usage, quality, safety, and people motivation) with no regard for profitability.

Plants in Japan had been managed as cost centers and not profit centers, thus, when domestic plant managers were assigned to overseas operations, they found it challenging to manage an operation such as Georgetown, as a profit center. (The top Japanese financial executive with whom I had worked at Georgetown told me that he added 10% ROA into company financial targets to emphasize the importance of asset control and asset turnover ratio on company profitability. He, too, was looking for a system to manage assets.)

Observing Toyota floor management, we saw that managers paid deep attention to cost-reduction activities that had been assigned to them, which could indeed have an impact on overall company profitability, but they generally paid no attention to how their own initiatives impacted profitability. And they certainly paid little attention to investment costs because those investments could actually boost labor productivity, making them look better on that score. Furthermore, perhaps due to the hubris that can come from being regarded so highly as leaders and TPS teachers by those outside of Japan, they had become complacent and ceased looking for new ways of seeing problems. They got used to the status quo and needed a stimulus to shake them up. When Toyota had very limited financial resources, Taiichi Ohno had developed three efficiency concepts: labor, material, and equipment. When Toyota became a cash-rich company, only labor efficiency thrived.

We decided to use ROA as a material and equipment efficiency index to connect production management and operations results with profitability, management of controllable items, and accountability for forecasting. The importance of ROA management is not merely to indicate a problem, but a means for management to identify risk factors and to prioritize where and how to better connect processes to profitability.

After introducing ROA as a KPI at the Tsutsumi plant, operations management became more eager to reduce assets, such as inventory and new capital investment. Reduction of inventory and capital investment is a cornerstone of lean manufacturing, but it can be difficult to convince managers to make those cuts on their own without a performance target to highlight their importance. A productivity measure does not do that—with productivity alone managers tend to want a generous investment allowance in order to run their operations smoothly without downtime and to push for higher productivity of direct operations.

ROA eventually became Toyota's worldwide method to review cost and asset performance. It stimulated business thinking among plant managements who had been given tasks of running operations with conditions such as production scheduling, equipment planning, and budgeting. These managers had tried to execute their tasks in the most efficient way, but they often did not pay enough attention to profitability—they claimed they could not be responsible for the financial result if external conditions or the forecast changed (e.g., how could they affect demand?).

For example in 2001, Tsutsumi launched a small multipurpose sedan with a 7,000 vehicles per month sales plan, but it sold only 4,000 per month. As a result, we loaned our extra workforce to a busier plant, slowed down our line speed, and added another minor model to the production lineup to compensate for some of the volume lost by the sedan.

Of course, newly invested equipment for the sedan was not fully depreciated and profitability plummeted, while cost-reduction targets performed as planned. That was good but not good enough: we needed extra cost reductions to offset this loss.

Managers argued that they had reduced costs as promised, and that the sedan-volume decrease and equipment investment (designed and approved by the production engineering division) were not their responsibility. They blamed the marketing forecast, mumbling that recent sales plans for new launches had been higher than they should have been, which had been hurting the plants.

We patiently listened, but then told them that there were no accurate sales plan on earth—all were eventually either higher or lower—so we had a reduced fixed cost and needed to absorb the downward fluctuation as an anticipated risk.

If actual sales were higher than planned, we would be busy trying to accommodate extra demand and earn higher profits. So how was it all right to ignore the volume decrease and accept lower profits? As Mr. Ohno told us: we must use equipment as fully as possible after it was depreciated because it was free, and equipment must be the target of kaizen to become more efficient for longer use.

At the time the Tsutsumi plant was suffering low volumes and produced many niche models because high-volume models had been transferred to a growing overseas production base. The plant was meeting performance targets, such as productivity, but volume was just 56% of the peak in 2000, and the plant would need much more investment to produce different models. The plant manager and management staff were justifiably concerned about their future and receptive to the idea of connecting their performance to a company profitability requirement (ROA) in order to secure their survival.

The plant's accounting staff calculated the current condition of the plant ROA, as well as shop-by-shop ROA in line with companywide ROA requirements (while clarifying internal transfer price between shops). Then we broke down ROA into asset turnover (further divided into fixed asset and inventory) and operating profit ratio (further divided into cost and sales) so that each shop management could understand the requirement—

reduction of both asset and cost. These were further divided into controllable indices such as shop-by-shop equipment investment to reduce fixed assets as well as operational indicators like equipment uptime to reduce investment on site.

Our ROA percentage was calculated by dividing operating profit by total assets. You can use net income instead of operating profit; we believed operating profit connected the index better with real operational problems (it is sometimes called "ROAM" or "return on assets managed").

ROA = Operating margin x Asset turnover ratio

$$\frac{\text{Operating profit}}{\text{Total assets}} = \frac{\text{Operating profit}}{\text{Sales}} \times \frac{\text{Sales}}{\text{Total assets}}$$

As with our productivity KPI, we used an ROA value tree. (See Appendices: *ROA Value Tree*) to break down the company target into operational requirements at lower levels. Each shop then developed their own tree diagram to connect their operation to their ROA targets. Now they could connect themselves to profit and asset turnover, which are essential TPS objectives: *lean assets with higher inventory turnover produced higher profit*. The plant's accounting department reported shop-by-shop ROA progress every month, which included profit, variable process cost, fixed cost, and asset balance. With this data, we started monthly review meetings for the plant manager, administration, and shop managers to discuss progress.

Plant management gradually began to understand how their actions contributed to companywide profit. The ROA value tree connected ROA with plant operations in a way that allowed management to realize potential or future problems, such as less demand than was forecasted. With an ROA target, all process management developed investment and current asset reduction activities that we followed with an operational KPI (in addition to our usual cost-reduction actions):

- Paint shop achieved equipment cycle time improvements that reduced new investment and scrap.

- Plastics shop improved injection-molding machine cycle time by 20%, and six pieces of equipment were transferred to another plant.

- Assembly reduced process inventory.

- Machine shop reduced inventory (e.g., extra tooling).

- Stamping improved lead time, which allowed it to reduce the inventory and number of stamping machines.

- All shops actively reviewed production engineering's new model investment plan and offered ideas to help engineers reduce investments.

As the result of those activities, they reduced $40 million in assets and another $40 million worth of new investments for the $5 billion Tsutsumi operation. Our annualized improvement in 2001 showed that ROA increased 39%, operating margin increased 26%, and the asset turnover rate increased 11%. With ROA as a guide, management understood how much they had to improve their operation to overcome potential economic downturns, and managers became conscious about investments and took actions to minimize them without impacting other performances (e.g., by using refurbished and/or reconfigured old equipment).

With this new ROA standard they found new problems. Given the difficult business environment in Tsutsumi and support from high-ranking Toyota officers, it was relatively easy to get management's buy in to ROA. Expansion of ROA management to other plants and operations, including overseas operations like Europe, however, required some effort.

Fortunately, I found an ally: the ROA system had been embraced by Toyota's TPS promotional office, which was famous in the lean world for developing and promoting TPS. They needed a theoretical explanation of TPS in order to further promote zero inventories against zero financial interest. They endorsed the ROA value tree and used it to explain TPS to others. With this support, ROA was elevated as a measure to show the progress of TPS and an important index to reveal problems related to fixed cost and assets.

Getting Started with ROA

To introduce an ROA system into a lean organization, get accounting to produce key data to calculate the current company-wide ROA as well as ROA for divisions/units, plants, and shops. (You also can opt to use allocated profit based on costs to see ROA trends.) Once you know current ROA, you can establish targets and begin to surface gaps (problems):

1. Set the ROA target based on how fast management expects to improve relative to benchmarked competitiveness. The company target is converted into division targets, unit target, plant target, etc. The company ROA target usually is smaller than the internal division target because it uses total assets as the denominator, including investment to other companies or securities. In this exercise you must be clear about inter-company transfer price, like product price from plant to sales for the calculation of ROA in each division or unit.

2. Break down the ROA target into operational second- and third-tier indices (ROA value tree). This will improve acceptance from your plant folks as the financial term becomes pragmatic to those who control items. This is a clarification of the cause-and-effect relationship, such as machine cycle time and die

change time. Understanding this relationship, plant-floor staff will try to improve cycle time and maintenance to avoid new investments.

3. Account for "risk," which can ruin good results if not properly managed. A financial target such as ROA can drive everyone to seek monetary results at the risk of harming fundamentals (e.g., safety, quality, and people development). Ensuring that risk factors are monitored will help to secure good, lasting financial results.

4. Align various budgets, including capital investment, with ROA targets to promptly judge progress by management. Most companies budget fixed and variable costs as well as capital investment, so the ROA target must be confirmed at each step of budget planning to balance costs and assets. When cost reduction is difficult, the asset control can be recognized as an alternative means to improve ROA. Once the fixed cost is budgeted by its category (including indirect labor, depreciation, maintenance, and other expenses), the standard for variable cost is established, and you can then predict the expected profit. Based on this prediction, asset turnover ratio should be established to meet the ROA target. If the ROA target for a plant is 50% and the operating profit ratio for the plant is budgeted at 10%, asset turnover ratio must be greater than 5.0. Usually fixed assets will not be reduced in a short period of time other than through depreciation; inventory should be your focus to improve the asset turnover ratio.

5. Insert all asset-reduction and cost-reduction plans and targets in your financial budget, and monitor the progress of these at least monthly. Because the budget is commonly followed and monitored at most companies, inclusion of asset-reduction plans will heighten visibility and, thus, present ROA and its relationship to asset reduction on a regular basis.

6. Make ROA information and data highly visible on an ongoing basis in order to identify problems quickly. Line managers must break down their responsible KPIs into daily operational KPIs, monitoring progress regularly and addressing problems immediately. These daily or even hourly operational controls of lower-tier indices are the real drivers to finding problems that can prevent reaching the overall ROA target.

Looking Ahead

In this chapter you learned about using strategy deployment and KPIs to establish a shared vision and how we applied systems for monitoring the effectiveness of hoshin management. You also got a glimpse at systems to identify problems with productivity and asset utilization that could prevent a lean vision from being reached. Like andon for leaders, they rapidly identify corporate problems before they severely impact outcomes.

But you will learn that successes in an organization can breed contentment. You will need to keep your organization challenged, especially when things appear to be going well. We will describe these challenges and how to overcome them in the next chapter.

Chapter 3 Key Questions

- Can you easily identify and share your company's vision?

- Is your company vision easily articulated by others throughout the company?

- How well do you, leadership, and members know your organization (value it delivers, mission, big and small, etc.)?

- Does your organization practice hoshin management to connect and compare long-term vision and should-be conditions to current conditions?

- Do you have a means to assess the effectiveness of your hoshin-management process?

- Do a handful of simple KPIs identify problem areas with your company's performance?

- Are companywide KPIs embraced and translated to lower-level KPIs and targets (e.g., for divisions, functions, departments, individuals)?

- Can you and others readily see and react to KPIs?

- What KPIs and systems to monitor them have proved most effective in your company?

4. Awake to See Problems

Georgetown Redux

Toyota Motor Manufacturing Kentucky (Georgetown) initially exceeded its targeted results and received much acclaim from the auto industry and business community. But there was a troubling trend behind the Georgetown success: for years the organization had been receiving substantial management expertise and support from Toyota Japan. Despite this support, performance began to deteriorate in the late-1990s.

By 2000 (since its startup in 1987), Georgetown had received 2,900 trainers and sent 700 trainees to Japan. In 2000, it needed another 200 headquarters-provided trainers to regain conditions that enabled it to achieve a J.D. Power and Associates Gold Plant designation. Toyota needed to redeploy these people around the world for its rapidly expanding Asia and China operations, which also meant they needed to move executives out of Kentucky. In addition to relocating trainers to other parts of the world, the best of the homegrown Georgetown management needed to take their knowledge to other parts of Toyota in North America. For this to happen, Toyota needed Georgetown to be self-reliant and continuously improve on its own.

But instead of improving, Georgetown had regressed after Mr. Cho's departure in 1994. Under Mr. Cho, it had received five plant awards from J.D. Power for five years in row: three gold, one silver, and one bronze. In the six years since his departure, it had received only one bronze award (1997).

In 1996, I returned to Kentucky after a three-year challenge to come up with a plan to reorganize North American operations to better fit into rapid global expansion. I executed the first step of the plan with Toyota Motor North America (still a paper company at that time, but evolving as originally planned) and Toyota Motor

Manufacturing North America, the manufacturing head office in Erlanger, KY. I became VP Corporate Planning of the head office to make sure it worked as planned. We chose Erlanger because of its location: a five minute drive from Cincinnati airport and an hour drive from the Georgetown plant. We carried out our vision to unify and reinforce North American manufacturing operations in Canada, Kentucky, and California; to ready the organization for immediate expansion in West Virginia and Indiana; and to prepare for future growth in Texas, Alabama, and Mississippi.

This took more time than expected. During that time, when trying to assist Georgetown, I encountered much resistance. They often refused to follow directions because they did not like the additional layer of management and they had become over-confident, despite the early signs of business deterioration. Leadership in Georgetown strongly opposed our guidance, and believed conditions would be enhanced if they were left alone. They did not want to see the problems they had, and instead cited outside issues. This was one reason that we developed KPIs in North America—to wake people up to see performance problems objectively at all facilities, including Georgetown.

At the beginning of 2000, after we made the North American manufacturing headquarters in Kentucky function as we planned, I returned to Toyota Japan, working with both Global Production Planning Division in the headquarters and Administration at the Tsutsumi plant, which was Georgetown's mother plant. While sending many trainers monthly, we discussed safety, quality, and productivity problems to improve their performance with Georgetown management. Even in these discussions, they often made excuses, such as saying they suffered from too much over-time to meet the KPIs. I knew that overtime at Georgetown was no more than at the UAW plants. They were looking for excuses for their poor results, avoiding seeing their problem squarely.

Despite this, with massive support from Tsutsumi plant Georgetown finally regained one gold award (2000) under the third new leadership, including chairman Masamoto Amezawa and president Gary Convis. Ironically, this gold award made things worse because it comforted management, which refused to recognize that they had a serious problem.

I was frustrated by Georgetown's complacency and their lack of true improvement. Equally frustrated was Shinichi Sasaki, who was a startup member of the UK Manufacturing company, which had similarly failed to become self-reliant. In 2000 and 2001, we worked together from the Tsutsumi plant to support Georgetown and the UK. We believed that these organizations had become complacent and that most of their leadership truly believed their plants were better than everyone else. They had been reading and believing their own press clippings.

Sasaki, who later became EVP of Toyota Japan, and I had discussed how the once brilliant operations had fallen to mediocrity after the first generation of leadership returned to Japan. We were supposed to have developed a kaizen culture and challenging spirit among local management, but the second generation of leadership had guided them to different places. We lamented the failure of continuous improvement. We had taught the local staff ourselves, showing what to do and why, but our coaching was not followed. In fact, we heard from local staff with whom we were still close that our coaching was being ignored or disrespected by the new generation of Japanese expats. Our colleagues were confused.

Sasaki and I discussed how long it would take to restore the original spirit into the third generation of leadership. We might need twice as long, since we'd also need time to wipe out the wrong culture that had developed with the second generation, in addition to restoring the original culture. Our problem was that Toyota headquarters had not established—in writing—what all the Toyota plants must pursue and what expats and locals must follow as the requirement in details. It was left to the individual leaders in charge of the plants.

The first generation of leaders had been the best choice because of the tremendous risk of each new project. But during this initial global expansion time, the leadership at the overseas plants changed periodically because Japanese expats returned to Japan after their assigned time, and local staff were changing their jobs frequently as well. How could we establish the system to instill the same management philosophy and methods among local staff and among our Toyota people in Japan, ending any confusion at the local level?

By many standards and compared to domestic competitors in each country, the plants were adequately run, efficient, and produced quality vehicles. Management and members regularly searched out and solved day-to-day operations problems. But instead of deep, self-sufficient problem solving that could lead to breakthrough gains, this was problem solving by numbers—working alongside and observing the Japanese expats and doing as advised. Occasionally they would stretch their problem solving capabilities, but rarely beyond a comfort level that simply was not enough to remain competitive.

Missing across Georgetown management was the nuance and knowledge of The Toyota Way, a level of understanding that even the expats there had begun to lose. The urgency of challenge and kaizen—truly required to be self-reliant—had all but disappeared. This was why Mr. Cho initiated compiling The Toyota Way. At the root of this problem was an inability to grasp the comprehensive management understanding at the level of detail needed to isolate and identify deeper problems, the kind of issues that could lead them to be competitive against any advanced Toyota plant anywhere.

We had taught this spirit when Georgetown was formed, and at one time the plant was nearly as good as the mother plant Tsutsumi, but we had not developed clear management standards in a way that would allow local staff to grow.

We decided to wake Georgetown up. I drafted a speech for Atsushi Niimi to address this concern at the plant in 2001. Niimi was one of initial expats in Georgetown, the plant manager of Tsutsumi, and later became EVP of Toyota Japan. He shared my concern, challenged Georgetown management, and identified unmet expectations:

You need two changes to be self-reliant; one is mentally and another is physically. Be aware that you have been in lukewarm water. You have been taking Tsutsumi protection for granted, and you are tapering off the spirit of challenge. See outside, like Sakichi Toyoda told his son, Kiichiro: 'Open the window, it's the big world out there.' You can see the dynamics in the fierce competition, and you can assess your performance. [Georgetown] is no longer the best, it is less flexible and higher in labor cost. With competitors and less buffer at Tsutsumi, you cannot avoid volume fluctuations. Do not be satisfied with the status quo, rather pursue relentless kaizen, the DNA of Toyota. Your initiative to success and pride only make it possible to be self-reliant. Create and maintain the sense of urgency for competition, and your endeavor succeeds in half the time. Then you have to manage the organization to strengthen its physical ability or skill. You should start with measuring them against benchmarks. Provide direction and target with a reward for achievement. But don't tell them what or how to do, rather let them take initiatives.

The speech made many individuals uncomfortable. They couldn't believe what they were being told and were unwilling to embrace the challenge. Two exceptions were Gary Convis (president of Georgetown, who had transferred from NUMMI in May 2000 and later became a Managing Officer of TMC) and Masamoto Amezawa (Georgetown's Chairman, who had helped it regain its gold status). They recognized that Georgetown was far from its best.

The next and more important step following the speech was to give leaders and management the means to better see their problems, see more problems, and to get better—the system to instill consistent management philosophies and methods. One way we did that was to develop and introduce Georgetown (and the UK) to a new way to assess their management processes and the extent to which those processes yielded desirable results. I lead this project with colleagues in Tsutsumi, we had outlined the minimum requirements as the standards that a manufacturing operation should have in place to be self-reliant for all aspects of manufacturing, including Plant Management, Accounting, HR, Quality Assurance, Procurement, Logistics, and Production Control. Against this standard, we could assess process and result of a plant to find problems.

In Japan, Toyota's geographically close locations and lifetime employment had developed a tacit knowledge base. Thus, we seldom documented key practices, instead we passed our knowledge from one generation to another by showing and practicing among ourselves. It was a critical error to presume this would occur outside Japan, where people had more diverse backgrounds, cultures, and languages. We learned of this system error through bad experiences like those at Georgetown and in the UK. For example, inconsistent training methodology: one trainer taught the same task differently from another trainer, which confused a trainee, even though the intent of the training was the same. We requested the unification of training methodologies and the use of the same trainer for a single subject.

The new assessment system was disseminated as our production management know-how through Toyota's Global Production Center located at the Motomachi plant in Toyota City and established in 2001 to unify the manufacturing method to be taught outside Japan. *The Toyota Way 2001* and the Global Production Center had been developed to manage global operations in the most efficient and effective way as one unified system. This was our most robust and comprehensive effort to date to standardize production management.

The self-administered assessment system looked at both process and results. The process assessment covered hoshin development, hoshin deployment, execution, kaizen, etc. The results assessment reviewed the ability of those processes to consistently hit KPIs and sub-KPIs, and the effectiveness of systems to support KPIs. The system guides managers through a PDCA cycle to develop a deeper understanding about the management processes in place, to determine the effectiveness of their management processes, and to form a consistent global understanding of The Toyota Way of manufacturing.

The assessment system initially was intended to develop the minimum requirements for mainly overseas plants, but trial assessments for plants inside of Japan revealed that the even the best Toyota plants could not hit the 100% mark; they were in the 75% to 80% range. This woke up Toyota management who also had become complacent and believed their plants in Japan did not have much room for improvement. Based on this evidence, management in Japan also set out to create problems that could be tracked, validated, and push plants to achieve improvements.

While I was in Europe, the Global Production Center had refined a standard assessment system for manufacturing plants inside and outside Japan. My colleagues in the Production Center reported that the assessment system was not initially embraced at Gcorgetown. Trial usage occurred in 2003; Georgetown departments assessed their processes as better than actual conditions warranted (even better than the Tsutsumi plant). But the real result assessment was significantly lower than Tsutsumi. This was a problem—Georgetown management thought that what they were doing what was acceptable even though they were not hitting the results that good processes should deliver. The rigor with which managers initially undertook assessments was also lacking. They were given a good problem-finding tool, but they casually used it.

Then they had a couple of critical breakthroughs, one from above management and one from within. President Convis and chairman Amezawa heavily promoted and championed the assessment system in 2004. They selected Cheryl Jones, then an assistant general manager for paint and plastics, to use the assessment system to its fullest—treat it as a true problem-finding tool and not just as a form to fill out.

Jones delivered her findings on use of the assessment system to a North America Production Joint Meeting in 2005. I had returned from Europe to the Erlanger head office at the end of 2004 to establish Team Member Development Center including North America Production Support Center. I was impressed with her presentation. She told us that the more she studied it, the lower her department scored; she had not understood the requirements deep enough at first. She was an original Group Leader hired in 1987. Before that, she had been a supervisor of a Kroger grocery store and had no experience in manufacturing. One department had been reluctant to hire her, but based upon my strong recommendation, the assembly shop picked her up and trained her. She proved to be very flexible and mastered many requirements as a production manager.

The deeper Jones got into evaluating her department on the requirements, drilling down through the assessment and evaluating supporting systems, the more she could see the department's scores getting worse. Layer by layer, she was seeing how systems were affecting performance and was able to identify problems and opportunities for improvement. (She eventually championed the assessment system and was promoted to VP Manufacturing at Georgetown.)

Once Jones' paint and plastics department was on board, improving systems and achieving results that did not exist elsewhere in Georgetown, other managers—expats and locals alike—recognized the value of the assessment system and used it to improve the way in which they managed and to surface latent problems throughout Georgetown. We continued to emphasize the need for self-reliance in North America to make up for the shortage of staff from Japan. Georgetown management gradually bought into the two-pronged assessment system, just as Jones had. By 2006, Georgetown was self-reliant; the expat management had fallen to one quarter from its peak time, and no trainers from Japan were on site in Kentucky.

Awake to See Problems

Every organization needs to be regularly and repeatedly challenged. Without keen awareness of an unattained vision or an unfulfilled dream, a corporation can become complacent. Even when reaching the top of an industry, without challenges there is a collective loss of motivation and energy and a once-formidable company can begin to decline. Without the constant pressure of an unattained vision to which leadership, management, and workers can strive, a good company will plateau and be overtaken by lesser competitors that continue to improve. Throughout history the list of companies that have toppled from lofty perches is long: Compaq, Daewoo, Lionel, LTV, Polaroid, etc. In today's hyper-competitive environment, the pace with which companies can close the gaps on industry leaders and send them tumbling is striking.

Senior leadership must regularly create and pose challenges in the form of an aspirational—often seemingly unobtainable—vision and provide the means for management and workers to move toward the vision. There needs to be a framework that regularly presents new challenges to the organization that are aligned to the vision, that expose problems (current condition vs. a better, should-be condition), and encourage management and the workforce to take calculated risks and experiment in the search for improvement.

The story of complacency in Georgetown is not uncommon. Without the means to establish a vision and more ambitious conditions and targets aligned with the vision, as well as the tools for management to constantly assess progress and alignment with hoshin (KPIs and a process assessment), any organization, including Toyota, can become complacent.

Since the inception of Toyota, we have believed that people embrace challenges and are more likely to enjoy working in a challenging but fair culture. It's not always a rosy path and there will be some in leadership and the workforce who resist. But it has been Toyota's philosophy since the 1960s—as evidenced by the introduction of TQC in 1961 and official hoshin deployment in 1963—that if leadership successfully shares a dream and vision among all members of the organization, people will pursue further improvements within their capacity for the organization and for their individual satisfaction.

Imagine an organization where no one is content with the status quo, no one is complacent, and where all members daily look for a better way to do their job. That is what we strived for at Toyota, and most days that is what occurred. Mr. Cho told us a story about Taiichi Ohno. When Mr. Cho tried to report on the progress of productivity for an operation, Mr. Ohno demanded that Mr. Cho go back and further improve it—despite having just achieved a 30 percent productivity improvement the day before.

Sure enough, Mr. Cho found another problem to solve on the operation and productivity improved again. Of course, Mr. Ohno then wanted to hear about the next improvement, not about the second improvement. In this way, Mr. Ohno taught him to never be satisfied with the status quo, which is the antithesis of kaizen. Mr. Cho once told me that he would rather be the president of the Toyota Supplier Support Center—the kaizen consultant group that worked with Toyota suppliers—than the president of Toyota Motor because he found kaizen so satisfying and that it renewed his spirit as a leader.

Top Toyota executives through the decades repeatedly created long-term visions to challenge and align the organization, starting with the dream more than 80 years ago to make an affordable car available for ordinary Japanese citizens. But as Toyota's ranks grew to more than 300,000 employees and its business spread through-out the world, alignment toward a shared vision and universal willingness to find new problems and accept new challenges became, itself, a challenge for Toyota.

Since the inception of Toyota, we believed
people embraced challenges and were more
likely to enjoy work in a challenging
but fair culture.

In searching to renew problem finding across the whole company, we identified a need to challenge management first, believing the workforce will follow management's behaviors. If management does not accept a challenge and break it down to the next level, others will not address the challenge either. Most companies have trouble getting their hoshin aligned beyond the executive level and through management and supervisors. We sought ways to cross this hoshin chasm.

To create a challenging environment at Toyota, three systems were regularly used to evaluate alignment of the organization around our shared vision and should-be conditions and to expose new problems. The first was our executive-level system to evaluate the effectiveness of hoshin deployment (explained in Chapter 3). The second, we used an assessment system at a site/location level to evaluate plant management processes and their ability to achieve results. The third tool was a visual board that challenged supervisors to regularly assess their role and their ability to achieve objectives within their control. Like mirrors reflecting real problems or new challenges, these systems helped corporate and site leadership bridge the hoshin corporate-to-plant floor gap.

The three systems have common principles—e.g., hoshin deployment, process and result control, KPI management, kaizen, and people development—and their application reflected how much Toyota was obsessed with consistently executing the same problem-finding approach throughout the organization and at all levels of the organization in a standardized manner. The systems enabled Toyota to align and reinvigorate its burgeoning global workforce, both inside Japan and in all countries of operation.

Such systems can help you to continuously challenge and force problem solving within your organization regardless of size or scope. They are mirrors for your organization. The constant, rigorous assessment in front of the mirror and against a standard reveals truths and problems. The mirror will not lie to you. At Toyota, these systems and the principles behind them established a framework to spur continuous improvement. But it is critical to note that had Toyota not tailored these systems for different levels of problems and problem-finding, it would have been difficult—or impossible—to share hoshin throughout the organization and a kaizen culture (thus, the three tiers of assessments). You and your management also must apply systems to solve big problems, with other systems to break those big problems down for each level of employment and to create new challenges for all levels.

Less complicated than these management systems, the three tools presented in this chapter—yokoten, benchmarking, and conditional challenge—will help you challenge your organization instantly, by creating problems that improve the organization. That doesn't occur if you simply find and solve a problem to preserve the current condition. Any improvement must become the new baseline *all across the company*. This is *yokoten*.

The best condition, though, rarely reside only inside of your company. As a leader, you must look elsewhere for challenges to your organization and must lead management to find *benchmarks* toward which your organization should strive. Lastly, *conditional challenges* (e.g., faster line speeds, less inventory, fewer workers), force management and staff to adapt to changing conditions, which quickly creates problems and forces management and employees to solve them.

Challenge Plant Managers with an Assessment System to Expose Their Problems

How does a successful organization, big or small, detail the measures and systems of its success and establish the baselines for further improvement? Can it even detail the measures and systems needed for success? Success would mean that all key performance indicators (KPIs) that support hoshin have been met or surpassed. Consequently, all second-tier KPIs—the drivers of those KPIs—are achieved, and subsequent tiers of KPIs are hitting their marks. Each of those KPIs should represent the new current condition, and the systems that deliver them represent the new standard. More importantly, all processes that produce the positive KPIs must be sustainable and adhere to the guiding principles of the company.

Given the myriad KPIs and processes that any company encompasses, regularly monitoring and then raising the bar on these elements can be a seemingly insurmountable obstacle to continuous improvement. Consider the example of pro golfers: they do not have to think about hand placement, shoulder position, feet placement, eye on the ball, follow through, etc., when hitting the ball. They do it instinctively through many repetitions and usually know when something is out of sync. Through repeated use of the assessment system, managers should develop this same type of intuition for detecting problems.

An assessment system also helps managers be proactive instead of a reactive when problem solving. Pro golfers know how various factors—slope of the fairway, wind, rain—will affect their swing before actually taking a swing, and they can be proactive in addressing these issues. Plant managers should look at sub-KPI trends and be proactive in heading off issues before they affect the main KPIs. It would be impossible for managers to control all KPIs and solve all of the problems in the shop. The goal of the assessment system is to make issues visual so managers can delegate tasks to subordinates, and also to train their subordinates on how to find and solve these issues on their own without being told to do it.

The Toyota Way 2001 and TPS established the founding principles of *how* a Toyota plant should be managed. But even those two cornerstones did not identify what an individual operation would and should look like going forward as it improves. Many capable overseas plants struggled to improve further or became complacent due to this lack of *should-be* plant details. Leadership in these facilities observed, discussed with colleagues at their mother plant, and understood should-be conditions on the surface, but they could not figure out what made the mother plant successful, even with the help of Japanese expats.

The plant assessment system that was used for Georgetown revitalization—called "plant management requirements" (PMR)—was designed to clarify the tacit knowledge of the plant management and assess the management processes and documents put in place to reach KPIs. From the assessment results, a numeric value was calculated and the areas that need further study were identified. Across global Toyota, the numeric value was used to identify the self-reliance of an operation—e.g., administrative, cost, production control, procurement, human resources, quality assurance, and production. As a self-evaluation, this numeric value also helped the local management identify problems that kept them from becoming self-reliant—note, though, it was not used for comparison of one plant against another. This was purposely done to encourage honest evaluations and to allow leadership to dig deeper and understand the requirements. Of course, if KPIs were low and the assessment score was high, this showed that the understanding of the requirements by local leadership was shallow, which was a deeper problem.

When there was a contrast between KPIs and assessments, it indicated that the local management did not fully understand the process requirement to produce a good result and/or did not properly assess the process. We developed supplemental documents to find the cause of poor results, and KPI trees to help them to connect a poor result to a poor process. When facing a score imbalance, we repeatedly asked them "whys" until they could see the omission of the facts or the cause of problem. (Mr. Ohno told us that we must ask "Why?" at least five times to find the facts—the famous *Five Whys* of Toyota.)

For example, once when we had serious quality problem, a manager told me that a worker did not follow the standardized work and thus produced a defect product. But the manager also asserted that other process requirements (e.g., hoshin sharing, training, check sheets, an andon, equipment maintenance, and poka-yoke) had been in place. Given that, I asked him why the worker could not follow the standardized work. We eventually found various causes for this after asking many *whys*: the regular worker had been replaced by a temporary worker on that day due to illness, additional quality checks had been added without allocating extra time for the shift because defects had been reaching the following process or the customer, the torque wrench was not maintained well, and so on. There was either no proper procedure on these issues or the proper procedure was not followed—a temporary worker training process, a standardized work-change procedure, an equipment maintenance procedure. The manager realized that he had done a poor job of completing the assessment and in fact finding.

The assessment system was instrumental in helping to ensure that the manufacturing centers around the world could attain and sustain self-reliance, a condition needed to align with the 2010 vision of 15% global market share. Without the self-reliance of the centers, Toyota would lack the expertise to launch new centers around the world and could not maintain the same quality and productivity as it expanded its production base. Assessments and self-reliance would also enable Toyota to develop global products for and by various countries and train all centers in an identical way with minimum resources because requirements were identical.

As an improvement approach, the plant assessment system drove management and workers to improve operational performance, including safety, quality, and productivity, and to reduce costs through kaizen. It forced manufacturing centers around the world to develop members in order to capitalize on their full potential and to utilize equipment and processes effectively in the same way, which meant that yokoten was easily understood by all plants. It also allowed for a major change in how business was allocated to plants. Previously, each manufacturing center was given new business (production volume) based on customer needs with no competition from within the company. After Toyota expanded in North America, the North American centers had to compete with each other for new business and the assessment system was a way to distribute new business.

When initially developed in Japan, the assessment system was labor-intensive and managers had to submit a lot of paperwork to make use of it. Its linear format made it difficult to easily connect sub-KPIs to main KPIs and to assess the current condition of the systems supporting the KPIs. Ted Agata improved the assessment framework to include the KPI-tree for operations areas and made it easier to use. The resulting assessment system focused on 10 elements that must always be known and controlled: safety, quality, production process, manpower, asset, cost, environmental compliance, maintenance, internal logistics, and *The Toyota Way*.

For your organization, even if it consists of just a single plant and self-reliance is not an issue, an assessment system can show what a high-performing operation should look like and establish gaps between that objective and current conditions. Managers describe the main system and the procedures and processes for management: establishing the mid-term vision and important policies (like environmental compliance), profit management (including profit, asset, and required cost reductions), and KPIs to be followed. It also describes a flow chart of operations to be managed with KPIs.

As assessment tree shows how KPIs (e.g., quality defect per product), second-tier KPIs (e.g., direct run ratio), and supporting systems (e.g., poka yoke) link together in an operations area. It allows managers to rapidly assess the state of their KPIs and supporting systems, and then break down those results, digging deeper to find real problems with systems that need attention. The assessment tree and overall system helps management to:

- Meet their goals.

- Proactively detect problems before they expand and impact main KPIs.

- Develop detailed understanding of the systems in their operations and make improvements to meet goals (kaizen).

- Recognize the requirement that they must go to the shop floor to get information and data necessary to complete the assessment (genchi genbutsu).

- Identify weak or missing systems, and determine which systems positively impact their operations and which ones need improvement.

The primary components of the assessment system are:

- *KPI tree* visualizes the links from KPIs to sub-KPIs and through systems examined as the 4Ms of Method, Manpower, Material, and Machine.

- *Procedure sheets* further help managers evaluate their systems by screening control items for each main KPI.

- *Handbook sheets* assist managers in identifying the point of cause of surface-level problems so that they can delegate subordinates to investigate root causes and solve these problems (and in the process train their subordinates on how to find and solve these issues on their own without being told to do it).

- *System summary sheets* use a radar-chart format to capture and communicate the current vs. should-be condition up and down the organization (see figure at right). It shows process points and total points, which are combination of process and result points by controlled items on each requirement category (e.g., safety, quality, cost, manpower).

Assessment System Summary

Once leadership identifies problems, they develop improvement plans and follow the plan as part of a new assessment or in establishing new hoshin items for the department. In this way the tools allow managers to assess the PDCA cycle of their systems. Hoshin and operations KPIs are the *Plan* phase of the assessment system. The *Do* phase is implementation of the system to monitor supporting systems (e.g., supervisor boards) that roll up to the operations-level assessment figures. The *Check* phase consists of the actual assessment tools to monitor how well systems function in meeting operations KPI goals. The *Action* phase is an improvement plan that emerges from the assessment work and that helps management determine what is needed to improve systems and how that should be reflected in future hoshin.

The following simple example shows the progression for *Check* and *Action* for an assessment for the quality branch of a KPI tree—you must check the existence of each item and examine the adequacy:

Main KPI: Number of recall items and number of defects

Recurrence prevention: Recall and defect prevention activity

4M: Method reliability of instructions and processes
(e.g., system for reflection and follow-up)

Material reliability (e.g., defect information from supplier)

Machine reliability (e.g., machine maintenance)

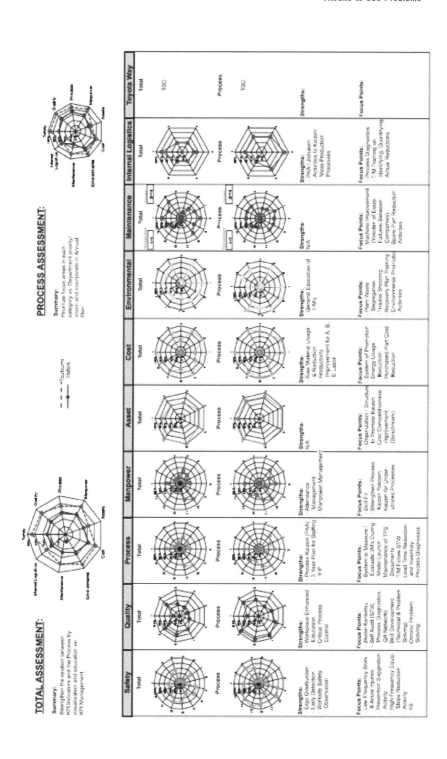

Manpower reliability (e.g., inspection training program)

Criteria and standards:

- Method (e.g., machine flow diagram)
- Material (e.g., list of items related to critical defects)
- Machine (e.g., machine check instructions, including poka-yoke)
- Manpower (e.g., human resources skills development).

Don't lose sight of the fact that Toyota's assessment system was designed to improve the way that managers think and to "strengthen their *thinking* way." Skill-development training was designed to improve a frontline worker's ability to detect problems intuitively. One of the goals of the assessment system was to also develop this type of problem-finding intuition for managers. Like an athlete who practices regularly to develop muscle memory, managers develop an intuition for detecting problems through repeated use of the assessment.

While some assessment requirements may seem impossible to stray from (e.g., kaizen and results analysis), development of subordinates is not always so top of mind for managers. They must be aware of these requirements until they became second nature. In fact, many managers told me that problem finding and solving became second nature, not just at work but at home as well. One manager in Canada sent me problem solving training material that he had developed by himself because he was obsessed with problem solving.

Managers who develop this kind of driven, problem finding intuition can see things more clearly and find deviations quicker. For example, when Teruyuki Minoura (who was the last disciple of Taiichi Ohno) visited Toyota Auto Body California as the president of Toyota's North American manufacturing operations, the first thing he did was check the metal sheets blanked on shelves to see the level of lot size (the smaller the better). With that simple check he could instantly see the die-change speed.

I, too, developed this intuitive sense. When I heard that the Georgetown body shop had achieved 100% run ratio one day, I asked my staff to check for any manipulation of the number. There had to be a problem because I was taught that a 100% run ratio meant too many people involved or something abnormal. Sure enough, they ran the operation faster than the planned speed to produce more auto bodies, but acted as if it were achieved with a 100% run ratio.

When we speak with company leaders and their managers, most understand the need to monitor detailed KPIs and systems, to work through the assessment progression to surface problems (even when none may be apparent), and to drive problem finding and solving out to staff. They get it. But what they often do not have or want to establish are the tools to measure and connect the KPIs and systems. That seems to be a daunting task for them, and it often is. Some companies have invested the time and energy to develop an assessment structure similar to that at Toyota. But many others have not, and for those—maybe you—there is good news.

You don't necessarily have to design your own assessment system or try to apply Toyota's assessment system as described here. You can adapt something you already have, for example, an ISO 9000 program. Many companies are required by customers to be ISO 9000 certified to get their business. If you have to do it anyway, you should take advantage of ISO 9000 because it contains a provision to assess for a sound management system that meets the needs of customers and stakeholders and assesses that quality is continuously improved. You can use the ISO 9000 or any similar framework as a basis for your assessment system, and expand it to other facets (e.g., costs, safety). Most important, though, treat the ISO or related assessments as a valuable, repeatable means to find problems, not merely an audit that is done and then shelved. What is important is its diligent, consistent usage, not the exact tool itself. Once you master a basic framework, you can develop your management requirements in more detail and more specific to your company.

Connecting Supervisors to Hoshin to Have Them Attack Their Problems

Executives often complain about how difficult it is to drive corporate objectives beyond senior management and down to middle managers and frontline supervisors. They recognize how important this group is to the hoshin process, but most are unsure of what requirements should be placed on supervisors in helping them to achieve hoshin objectives. And not knowing precisely what supervisors should do, it's difficult to engage them in problem finding and connect their actions with hoshin.

When we taught how to deploy hoshin to executives in North America and Europe and at our suppliers, most executives regarded hoshin as high-level policy. They did not see it as a method for line supervisors, although they recognized the need of lower-level participation. Therefore, even in Toyota, they tended to leave what to do about hoshin for supervisors in the manager's hands—providing them with no structural approach.

With no structure, we found it difficult to teach frontline supervisors their role in the hoshin process. They felt that hoshin was above their level and not the responsibility of any one person, especially one of them. The supervisor position is traditionally considered to be just a "watchman," but we wanted supervisors to develop people and be more open to improving their own way of working. Frequently supervisors told me that they understood what was required of them, but they would complain that their managers demanded too much of them: they were responsible for production, people development, safety, quality, environmental issues, etc. "Everything is on my shoulders."

This was the supervisor's burden, and we took it as our challenge to break them of this mind set. How can we develop supervisors and smooth out and streamline the requirements of their role so that they can support management requirements and department hoshin, which in turn, supports us and corporate hoshin? It also was difficult for management to know if line supervisors were performing their roles in a standardized manner targeted toward hoshin. We needed to bring supervisors into the improvement hierarchy.

At the beginning of Georgetown, Toyota Japan provided various training tools to help develop supervisors, such as videos depicting the supervisor's role and one-day activities to develop best practices. Nonetheless, we still struggled for a solution to do this effectively. About 2003, Toyota came up with the concept of a *supervisor visual board* that helped us grasp what was being controlled (management condition/management focus) and group development needs. This was an exhaustive piece of work based on actual practice of a veteran supervisor.

We liked the concept but not the meticulousness of the board, so the North America Production Support Center created a condensed version. We called it a "floor development management system" (FMDS). It showed supervisors people-development issues and performance issues (e.g., production, quality, safety) in conjunction with manufacturing department hoshin. Importantly, it offered a standardized way for supervisors to manage the information on the board.

Finally, we had found a way for the company hoshin to be connected to frontline supervisors and for them and everyone under them to manage daily work in support of their managers' hoshin. Most important, the board highlighted problems that previously had not been regarded as problems. Because hoshin demanded that supervisors improve current conditions or to try to change the standard, this triggered a need for kaizen at the base of manufacturing.

The FMDS board had become a comprehensive system to align floor management and development activities in order to achieve company targets and support the assessment system KPIs and systems that support KPIs. By doing this, you can:

- Ensure foundational skills are in place for supervisors so they can capably perform their work

- Align shop-floor activities with hoshin goals and objectives

- Visually demonstrate the management condition of the shop and alignment of daily activities to hoshin targets

- Promote two-way communication in order to address abnormal conditions through targeted problem solving, to determine needed support and resources, and to develop team members

- Define and develop roles and responsibilities for all team members.

At our North American manufacturing companies, the supervisor board and the method to manage it provided a highly effective, visual management framework that communicated clear targets and expectations to supervisors. It enabled companies to progress toward the higher performances necessary for the self-reliance that we were seeking. While I was in Europe, we tested the original version of the board at Toyota Poland to improve supervisor's activities and then confirmed the effectiveness of the supervisor board throughout Europe.

A huge benefit of the board was that it made supervisors' jobs easier, which freed up more of their time to develop the skills and abilities of manufacturing team members. Too often, supervisor practices had focused solely on managing daily production issues at the expense of spending time developing people. This was our breakthrough—it is the daily opportunities to develop people on the job that make for effective supervisors and lasting and effective shop-floor management. Not only did we help standardize supervisor activities and guide them toward hoshin, we made a big leap in developing a kaizen culture in our North American companies.

Many of the concepts necessary to implement the supervisor board in your organization are probably already in place, as they were at Georgetown. It is how you organize and sequence them that will begin to drive hoshin into your supervisor levels:

1. Demonstrate to supervisors that floor management fundamentals are in place using 5S, standard work activities, etc. This indicates readiness for the board. Without basic rules to ensure safety, quality, productivity, cost, and people development, as measured by the 5S level or presence of standardized work, the group will not be successful using the supervisor board. For example, if the workplace is not well-organized according 5S criteria, the group must implement 5S prior to putting the board in place. Likewise, if standardized worksheets are not established properly—including required knowledge, skill, and elements of the work and the role and responsibilities of the group leader and team leader to manage the standardized work—the group must establish these basics.

2. Translate hoshin into measurable objectives for supervisors to get across an understanding of what is expected, the basic behaviors they should exhibit, and the actions necessary to:
    - Ensure safety of all team members
    - Build quality into the product or service
    - Achieve production targets
    - Manage cost
    - Developing a strong, flexible workforce.

3. Build a visual system to measure and track activities and to identify abnormal conditions:

- Analyze and understand hoshin at the shop-floor level

- Set up supervisor expectations by identifying targets (KPIs, sub-KPIs, and processes)

- Evaluate daily activities to determine appropriate preventative activities to achieve targets

- Create the visual management system that incorporates this information.

4. Assess effectiveness in utilizing the supervisor board and assessment tools:

- Track to see if supervisor adherence is rolling up toward broader objectives and impacting plant assessments.

- Confirm that supervisors are using an assessment sheet to determine their own performance levels.

- Routinely clarify the role of the supervisor to determine if some aspect is missing or misunderstood.

- Assess supervisors' capabilities at problem finding and solving, including application of effective decision-making and problem solving (based on their visual confirmations of impact on KPIs), use of real-time feedback on the effectiveness of countermeasure activities, and their development of front-line staff through on-the-job training.

5. Develop a plan for each supervisor and provide ongoing coaching. At Georgetown, plans were developed by managers and assistant managers, who were responsible for developing their own staff through day-to-day, on-the-job training (i.e., coaching).

The supervisor board process is governed by PDCA. The *Plan* phase begins with the corporate hoshin and department hoshin. The daily use of the board and tools by the supervisor to manage the shop floor is the *Do*. The *Check* phase consists of the supervisor's assessment sheet, which management uses to check if a supervisor has the correct systems in operation and the effectiveness of those systems. *Action* is the supervisor's development plan, mapped out in conjunction with management.

Three Ways to Establish Should-Be Condition

The plant assessment system and supervisor board enable you and management to find problems that prevent your organization from achieving its shared vision. They also establish the guidelines to delegate problem finding to subordinates and will lead them to pursue problems on their own. We emphasize PDCA in describing both tools because without this emphasis you simply solve the same problems over and over, or you eliminate one level of problems and become complacent. That is a dangerous position. There are no problems. There is nothing to fix. Life is good.

Life may be good, but it's probably better somewhere else—inside your organization or outside of it. Yokoten, benchmarking, and conditional challenges are ways by which to systematize the capture of better ideas and develop new baselines, new should-be statuses for your organization.

Yokoten, benchmarking, and conditional challenges are ways by which to systematize the capture of better ideas and develop new baselines, new should-be statuses for your organization.

Yokoten

Yokoten (Japanese for horizontal deployment or adoption) means that when a better idea or process for better performance is developed, tested, and confirmed, it becomes the new target that a similar or comparable operation must hit or emulate. To proceed any other way—unless it surpasses the new target and is a better idea or process—is wrong.

Yokoten creates challenges or competitions among similar or comparable operations, getting them to achieve best performance because one operation has already achieved the best and shown how to do it. Those operations that cannot keep up are suddenly in the spotlight—their problems are found and can be addressed.

Toyota used yokoten when we had to establish standards for a new model development, as previously mentioned for setting up a new productivity standard. Yokoten also was used to judge the performances of similar operations in combination with relative evaluations. Relative evaluations are rankings of managers on criteria such as safety, quality, productivity, or other internal competitions. This also included quality-circle competitions to gage their ability to develop their people. Yokoten pulled up performances across Toyota, created new best conditions as managers sought to keep their operations above the high mark, and pushed all managers to be more competitive.

We encouraged similar or comparable operations to adopt yokoten, but the management of many such operations were reluctant to emulate what others had achieved (they suffered from the "not invented here" syndrome). They did not want to follow others, and would rather come up with a better idea on their own in order to be recognized by their executives. This attitude was not necessarily bad as long as they competed against each other to develop further challenges.

Toyota developed a database to inform managers of new ideas for the best performance. This is where managers looked for yokoten among comparable operations. When implemented, these ideas usually resulted in better performances immediately. But usage of yokoten was slow to disseminate better ideas across the organization. We even pooled resources at Tsutsumi to encourage use of yokoten and to eliminate the excuse not to implement a better idea. Yokoten can be challenging to get buy-in, as was the case with Toyota, but we still encourage you to use it to develop new standards.

Benchmarking

Rarely if ever today do best practices and best performances come from within one company. You may think your operations, products, and customers are highly unique to your organization and there can be no external comparisons that might shed light on a better way. Trust me, they exist. If you can find competitors or competing ideas, you will find problems in your company.

In many industries *external benchmarks* are readily available. For example, at Toyota we would use the J.D. Power Initial Quality Survey and similar external rankings to establish evaluation measures for managers, driving them to not only achieve the Toyota best but the industry best. You could also learn how good you and your competitors are from customer feedback on your product or services

At Toyota, when evaluating managers, we weighed their problem-finding abilities relative to hoshin targets and external benchmarks. Were they changing their approach to address new problems? This is a clear example where should-be conditions and problem finding are integrated into the performance management system. If the should-be condition or vision does not have an impact on the individual and/or vice versa, then it will not be perceived as important enough to be considered a serious matter by management.

Management can set long-range objectives as a vision to unify members, such as "No. 1 in your industry," but leadership must also help to define what being "No. 1" means by benchmarking and closely examining competitors. Of course, if you get to No. 1, you set another vision linked to should-be status for further improvement.

Conditional Challenges

Have you ever faced a suddenly challenging situation, been forced to come up with a new way to work, and then wondered why you didn't always do it that way?

Conditional challenges allow management to uncover their own organization's threshold of performance by forcing them to run their business under more challenging conditions, e.g., faster line speeds, less inventory, fewer employees in the office. Without the buffers of excess, bottlenecks and problems rapidly emerge, and managers must stop the operation frequently and address the problem—a problem they would not have encountered otherwise.

Toyota plants used a tactic, called the "one-second challenge" for line speed changes because problems emerged so quickly even one-second faster. A large-scale example of this occurred in 1993, when Toyota reduced headcount outside of manufacturing by 5%, and shifted these resources to other areas to solve tasks that had been regarded as important but had been placed on the back burner due to manpower constraints. (These were talented people with the ability to tackle difficult problems who were relocated.) This created a conditional challenge for the rest of business to improve operational efficiency because they must maintain the same service or tasks with less manpower (95%).

Toyota called this effort *business reform*, and since then has developed many business reform tasks as a way to constantly challenge current conditions. Conditional challenge must not, though, put customer deliveries in danger, or place overburden (or muri) on workers.

Once you identify weak operations you either fix the problem immediately or you go back to a slow speed if you cannot fix the problem right away. The key was that we usually would not have identified the problem to be fixed and would not have fixed it unless we had developed a conditional challenge.

Yokoten, benchmarks, and conditional challenges also prove enlightening to senior leadership. The story of my experience in Europe is a good example. As you may recall, the financial situation for Europe Manufacturing was not good. So I first broke down the surface problem into *sales* and *cost*, because profit equals sales minus cost. I then further broke down each into subcategories: sales into price and volume by models and countries, and cost into categories like depreciation, labor, material, interest, inventory, and so on, by products, plants, offices, and countries. Only after subproblems were investigated against internal and external benchmarks did we really identify our two biggest problems: depreciation cost for manufacturing and pricing for sales.

Three-shift operations were introduced in our French and Polish plants as one countermeasure to reduce depreciation cost. But the price problem was not well addressed. The price for our products was much lower than our competitors with equivalent specifications, but only a handful of countries were making money.

Our request to the Sales & Marketing group—raise the price comparable to competitors—was not accepted. The sales group reasoned that we did not have the brand power of our competitors. They made the price problem rather vague, instead of breaking down price itself by market, by age of the product, by engine etc. to see real problems against benchmarks.

The reaction of the Sales & Marketing group then made us convert the low-price problem to a problem of lack of brand power, which was a challenge that existed for many years within European Toyota. Toyota gradually challenged the brand-power issue, such as by participating in Formula One racing from 2002 to 2009. With greater brand awareness came step-by-step price increases. However, we never resolved the problem completely because the brand issue was too vague, subjective, and difficult to reach root causes.

Without finding a real problem, no one can really solve it. We encourage you to build genuine mirrors like the systems and tools described in this chapter by which to constantly examine your organization. They will enable you to create problems that were not previously known. And when those problems are visible and found, you, your managers, and your supervisors will find it difficult or impossible to remain complacent.

Looking Ahead

In lean management it is necessary to present people with constant challenges or problems to be solved *in their capacity*. That is why in the course of this book we have worked through the organization, carrying the hoshin message to management and supervisors and aligning it with roles and responsibilities for which they are capable. Leadership is the most responsible party in this endeavor, with the obligation to guide members of the organization. This includes providing a vision, its conditions and standards as a mirror to awake each member to see their problems; clarifying the value of what they are responsible for; providing them with the proper means to accomplish their tasks; and leading, coaching and, when necessary, telling them what to do. Ultimately, your role is to challenge people to do better in accomplishing the shared vision of the organization.

In the next and final chapter, we look ahead by looking back, briefly reviewing the essentials necessary to establish and improve a problem finding culture—but doing so in a context of what *you* should do first in *your* company.

Not every organization starts from the same level of problem finding preparedness. What can quickly accelerate a kaizen culture in one company may be redundant or too advanced in another. In addition, we will identify some of the biggest barriers that you and your management team are likely to encounter as you lead a problem finding culture toward your shared vision.

Chapter 4—Key Questions

• Does your organization have an ability to regularly assess management processes at a plant level and the effectiveness of those processes?

• Do supervisors have a clear and simple way to understand their roles and how the actions they take are helping—or hurting—the organization.

• Are managers willing to share good ideas, and as important, are they willing to accept a good idea that is not their own?

• Can you identify the best performances among your competitors? Have you tried?

• What would happen in your organization if you applied a conditional challenge, such as removing workers (deploying them elsewhere) or inventory from a process? What would you learn if you did?

Your Lean Journey

The needs of organizations moving further on their lean journeys and developing kaizen cultures capable of finding and solving *any problem* depends on where their leaders believe their businesses stand today. Are you looking for the concepts and ideas that can push your company along and overcome a period of stalled progress? Are you looking to start your journey and find and reach the first lean milestone? Have you lost the lean path with managers and employees confused by a mish-mash of tools and techniques and without a cohesive philosophy or basic thinking to guide your way?

The matrix on the pages 146–147 shows a way to understand organizations based on their status as they proceed along a lean journey, according to the levels of adoption of lean thinking, concepts, tools, and systems. Lean progress becomes more advanced as you move from left to right on the matrix. For each organizational status, I suggest a sequence of milestone activities to improve organizational performance and kaizen culture. I also describe the challenges you are likely to encounter as you move along an idealized path.

Note that the flow for each organizational status starts with or incorporates ongoing activities: 1) vision and mission, 2) commit to and communication of mutual trust and respect, 3) common value reinforcement, and 4) people development. Operationally, each company has countless specific problems to address as well as principles and processes to learn and apply. But, these four organizational staples must be present if you wish to create a kaizen culture. That is: IF YOU WISH. Without these four, any desires or ambitious statements about establishing a kaizen culture will be a waste of your time and the time of everyone in your organization. Just don't even bother.

Sequencing Your Lean Journey

Corporate Status	Little or no lean		Some lean tools and techniques	Full lean systems	Advanced lean
	Brownfield	Greenfield			
Problems >>	Old practices against lean	Can absorb anything	Need corporate-wide kaizen efforts	Avoid complacency	Keep eternal motivation to kaizen
Core Belief					
Vision and mission	1	1	Ongoing	Ongoing	Ongoing
Commit to and communicate mutual trust and respect	2	2	Ongoing	Ongoing	Ongoing
Common value reinforcement; no problem no kaizen	3	3	Ongoing	Ongoing	Ongoing
People development	4	4	Ongoing	Ongoing	Ongoing
Management Major Initiatives					
Hoshin management aligned with shared vision	TBD	TBD	1	Ongoing	Ongoing
Lean tools	5	5	Ongoing	Ongoing	Ongoing
Flexible work practices	6	6	Ongoing	Ongoing	Ongoing
Common problem-solving method	7	7	Ongoing	Ongoing	Ongoing
Promotion departments	TBD	TBD	3	Ongoing	Ongoing
Ongoing Measurement Tools					
KPIs and KPI trees	TBD	TBD	4	Ongoing	Ongoing
Return on assets (ROA) management	TBD	TBD	TBD	5	Ongoing
Periodic Assessment (Mirrors)					
ISO9000 or comparable	TBD	TBD	TBD	2	Ongoing
Hoshin assessment system	TBD	TBD	TBD	3	Ongoing
Manager and supervisor requirements	TBD	TBD	TBD	4	Ongoing
Competitive environment					
Production efficiency measure	TBD	TBD	5	Ongoing	Ongoing
Yokoten	TBD	TBD	6	Ongoing	Ongoing
Benchmarking	TBD	TBD	TBD	6	Ongoing
Conditional challenges	TBD	TBD	TBD	6	Ongoing
Self Satisfaction					
Align incentives and appraisals with problem finding culture	TBD	TBD	TBD	1	Ongoing
Rewards and recognitions	8	TBD	2	Ongoing	Ongoing
Suggestion system	TBD	TBD	7	Ongoing	Ongoing
Self-motivated problem finding (e.g., quality circles)	TBD	TBD	TBD	7	Ongoing

Little or No Lean in Brownfield

Leading a brownfield company or plant with little or no lean is not an enviable position, but not uncommon where a company or plant is losing competitiveness because it has been sticking to the status quo and old practices. This is typical when a majority of management or the rank and file are unwilling or unable to see their problems because they are blinded by their past success. We saw such conditions in older GM plants where management had rejected lean concepts or where they and the union were reluctant to change. Old practices—mass-production methods with rigid work rules—worked against lean and favored the status quo. In these settings, it is imperative to find and clarify problems and convince everyone of the seriousness of the problems.

This condition also occurs when organizations are acquired, such as when a private equity firm buys a company and replaces its leadership. Many such firms become rudderless; they lack a vision and mission (beyond making money) or both are outdated. They have no North Star by which their leaders or employees can navigate and no discernible value that all were willing to share. Conditions may have deteriorated to an adversarial workplace (union or non-union) and just getting to zero is necessary before a lean foothold and the actual journey can begin.

In such settings, it is so critical to work on developing *mutual trust and respect*, particularly if new leadership is on the scene. There must be some common ground from which management and employees can move forward as a team. People have to feel that management values them as more than material and labor. Without some modicum of mutual trust and respect, employees won't see the vision and they won't share a value—they may recognize the value, but they will see it as management objectives that will not enhance their fortunes.

As we learned when getting NUMMI underway, without trust and respect it will be difficult to make the large, necessary process changes that allow a problem-finding culture to flourish (e.g., development of flexible work practices) and the incorporation of new lean tools and techniques will be viewed suspiciously as cost- and labor-cutting mechanisms.

At NUMMI we took advantage of the management change from GM to Toyota to break old practices and we gained an innovative labor contract to spell out the vision and mission. We developed mutual trust and respect not only within the contract language, but also from management's response to labor, such as giving access to andon cords to stop the entire operation (a previously unheard of option within GM).

In contrast, Toyota struggled to implement its lean system in Australia a few years *before* NUMMI due to an old union contract and lack of trust. Union members often walked out to oppose new systems being implemented. What was lacking was the understanding that harmonious labor relations based on mutual trust and respect are necessary. Leadership also believed that people management could and should be done by local management, who knew local practices better than expats. Thus, there was no Toyota HR executive on location to explain the need for flexible work practices, show the rank and file how this could improve their work, and elicit some agreement for using flexible work practices. Without this role, management was unable to pioneer a path toward mutual trust and respect.

One activity that can help you with this challenge is the development of a *rewards and recognition program*. Meaningful incentives can help to dissolve years of adversarial history and provide concrete proof that "We're in it together." The right incentive helps to get people to learn about and apply lean tools and trust that their problem finding and solving can result in personal as well as corporate good.

In NUMMI, we promised job security to the highest extent possible; we spelled out that we would pull back outsourced jobs or reduce management compensation before we would consider layoffs. And we eliminated the management-only cafeteria and the management-only parking spaces to show respect to our members. Every morning, workers saw president Toyoda walking to his office with them and every lunch time, they saw the president eating the same meal with them at the same cafeteria. Workers felt the change and were willing to respect one another.

Once you solve the problem of old practices blocking your lean journey, you can then introduce lean tools and a common problem-solving method, focusing your efforts around people development— gradually building a workforce that is both eager and *able* to find and solve problems.

Without lean tools and the means to find and solve problems, your lean journey will not start. You will have an organization confused by the processes thrown at it. Management and the workforce will rapidly retreat toward old practices before anyone even understands the need for change. At NUMMI, we sent floor leaders to Japan for training with lean tools and a common problem-solving method for kaizen. In return they committed to train team members and act as teachers in the United States alongside our Japanese trainers. And we continued to reinforce their learning with problem-solving training.

Little or No Lean in Greenfield

The great opportunity that a greenfield operation presents is that of establishing vision, mission, and corporate culture with a management team and a workforce that you design. You have the opportunity to draw your ideal company or plant on a blank canvas, staffing precisely those who will support ideal conditions. Of course, this also represents the biggest challenge in that you start, literally, at zero: no employees, no culture, no kaizen. The problem is that you can go anywhere, right or wrong.

There are good examples of how it can go wrong: Saturn Corp. started its greenfield operation in Tennessee close to the time that Toyota began in Kentucky. Both had strong vision and mission, committed and communicated mutual trust and respect, spent enormous amounts of time on training, and established a common value. Each had flexible work practices and lean tools for production. Both had initial success but ended up with completely different results. Thomas A. Kochan of MIT reported in 1999 about Saturn:

> The parties have been caught in a downward, reinforcing spiral. The union was frustrated with a *lack of leadership and decision-making power within Saturn management* ... At the work place, the partnership was put on hold. Workers, in turn, became demoralized as they saw sales and production fall; as the relationship deteriorated, they began falling into traditional patterns. Therefore, performance declined, adding further to costs and the frustration of management.[4]

In 2004, the unique and original concept of Saturn was voted down by workers by a three-to-one ratio, and by 2010, the company had gone out of business due to its poor performance. Saturn's mutual trust was designed to have joint decision-making between union, workers, and management. Different from Toyota's belief and execution, management did not carry out their decision-making responsibility and instead, pushed it on to workers beyond their capabilities. People *will not* enjoy problem solving beyond their capabilities. Therefore, mutual respect disappeared and any remaining trust evaporated when the business went downhill. You must pick the right path at the very beginning to succeed on your lean journey that begins at a greenfield setting.

As for introducing management and the workforce to lean tools or problem-solving techniques, if you do not have good knowledge in house, hire top-class expertise or consultants who

4. Thomas A. Kochan, *Task Force Working Paper #WP09*, Institute for Work and Employment Research, Sloan School of Management, MIT, May 1, 1999.

understand the background of lean—not just technically but also philosophically—to promote not only tools and technique, but also the common value of problem finding for kaizen. As we learned from at Georgetown, you should recruit candidates with the right cognitive and physical abilities. With such a group you can develop a positive corporate culture, introducing them to broader tools built upon your core beliefs, and steadily advance your lean journey.

Your leadership challenge is to rapidly build lean experience and an organization-development function to instill common values to all employees. It is precisely because of this that understanding and acquiring *lean tools* and *problem-solving techniques* are the two most important pieces to get in place for a greenfield operation.

Some Lean Tools and Techniques

You may have noticed that hoshin management was absent in the sequence of activities for greenfields and lowest-level brownfields. That's because management and employees must digest the core thinking first and flex their lean muscles, use tools and concepts, and learn to find and solve problems that are behind the plan or current standards at their operations. This basic stability is important to maintain basic planned performance, which alone is difficult for many organizations.

As your staff and workforce gain experience, your problem becomes one of how to advance the lean journey still farther. It's at this stage that one part of the company may work well with the lean system and solve problems in their operation, while others are not as successful and corporate-wide problems go unsolved or more importantly, go unnoticed. This is the point where you and your management are eager to extend success companywide but may be frustrated by a large problem—failing to understand where it originates or how to begin to address it. The problem lacks context. Why is it a problem?

As the leader, you must establish and communicate that context with a mid-term vision and annual hoshin that will guide the organization in seeing and finding problems that contribute to the corporate problem. Management and the workforce will collectively and effectively tackle the big problem through their individual contributions. They all grow into "a company" and as a company can pursue your clearly articulated hoshin that cascades down through the organization.

If you try to roll out hoshin management too early in an organization's lean journey, people simply won't see the targets and objectives as their own—it is management just throwing up objectives and they won't make the connection. Not until people have had sufficient experience in finding their own problems and in taking responsibility for their roles and overall contributions are they likely to embrace the idea of a leadership and planning infrastructure that reaches down to their individual roles. It is also at this stage that their own problem-solving experiences begin to bump into bigger problems. The causes they encounter when finding problems may be tied to a corporate policy or practice that the individual alone could not solve or change. With hoshin management you will give them a big picture of what "we will accomplish as a company" and the freedom to take on broader problems and pull in resources they need to solve the problems they find. At this level of kaizen culture, individuals pursue the ideal condition of the *organization*.

Many executives find their companies at this transitory stage of development: some successes through lean initiatives, modest and disparate performance improvements around the company, and a challenge to sustain the successes that have been achieved. Naturally, top management wants to expand success across the organization and involve more people. Companywide initiatives, like hoshin, must be deployed to lend direction for future improvements. Designating a promotion department for each initiative may help to instill the initiative in all departments. The promotion departments will consistently communicate objectives associated with the initiatives and provide support and learning as new hurdles are hit in trying to achieve and sustain initiatives.

Once many companywide initiatives have been deployed, you begin to monitor ongoing performance to gauge their effectiveness and assess if problems are being clearly seen by everyone. A set of KPIs (or single KPI like production efficiency) will be effective tools to evaluate performance. A KPI tree will provide them with the speed to identify problems in order to advance their lean system.

You also will need systems to encourage and motivate employees to reach the higher goals being set forward: The competitive environment enhanced by KPIs, yokoten methods, and rewards and recognitions give employees reason to continue what they've been doing and to step up their involvement. These tools—combined with a suggestion system—encourage more individual problem-solving efforts and improvements aligned toward a shared corporate-wide vision.

Full Lean System

If your organization is at a stage that has implemented most of the lean tools, techniques, and systems on the matrix, chances are that you are not even reading this book. You may wonder why others are not writing books about you and your organization. You should be proud of the success your organization has achieved, but the moment of pride should and will last for only a brief moment.

Unfortunately, most everyone else in the company will also have these same feelings of success and pride. The last thing anyone in the company will want or expect is criticism, either internally from leadership or from outside the organization. Celebration and feelings of pride can contribute to enthusiasm and provide motivation. But in such times, it will be your job to throw proud thoughts out on their ear before they sow the seeds of complacency. Difficult, but that's exactly what you should do.

Your first objective here is to align appraisal and incentives with the culture of problem finding and continuous improvement. Whether or not management likes the problem finding and continuous improvement culture, it must be reinforced. Few executives will feel complacent when they understand that their advancement and even employment is governed by a system of meritocracy tied to continuous improvement.

Another objective is to establish mirrors for your organization so that management and workforce can see how much more improvement is not just possible but necessary. Here you will rely on the periodic and consistent evaluation systems to strengthen ties to aggressive hoshin objectives, corporate to plant floor. You must crack the complacency that sets into a good-but-not-great company. You should also establish linkages between financial targets and operational targets—e.g., return on asset management (ROA)—to measure how far the lean system must advance to achieve financial goals.

Another objective will be to look beyond your company for motivation. Benchmarking is critical to identify a frontrunner for every aspect of your business. Through trade associations, market research, or special studies conducted by various organizations or government agencies, you can find benchmarks and identify a gap between your current condition and those of leading competitors.

Also common is to tap into performance rankings that show how your organization stacks up to others in your industry. Toyota used J.D. Power and Harbour Report data as constant benchmarking sources, presenting a perspective of the organization from the outside looking in. Competitive data allows you to see your company as others see you. Today you can add social media, with the ability of consumers to "like" organizations, as another means to provide an external view.

But expect to hear naysayers when you present benchmark findings to others, as we did at Georgetown when performance there reached a plateau. Some will ignore you; others will question the methodology of the sources. The excuses will vary, but if you are consistent and relentless in holding up the mirrors, eventually the true face of your organization appears and others will finally see problems again.

Some companies have brought external benchmarks in house, pulling in a senior executive with a track record of superior performance. Ford Motor Co. did this in 2006 when it brought in Alan Mullaly from Boeing, where he was credited with leading the manufacturer's resurgence, and similarly, he led Ford to an extraordinary transformation during his tenure there.

When you reach this stage of your journey with a full lean system, you also should launch and support *self-motivated problem finding teams*. Grassroot group activities improve self-satisfaction among your most motivated people and epitomize kaizen culture.

Advanced Lean

No company has ever reached and sustained the state of a truly advanced lean organization. Problems will still need to be found and solved. Not even Toyota has achieved this advanced lean status. Perhaps they are close and hopefully will continue to strive for this level, but there are so many areas where—in my view—management and the workforce may have forgotten problem-finding and continuous improvement or kaizen. With more than 300,000 employees worldwide, it is very difficult to fulfill and sustain all requirements without complacency for any organization, particularly mutual trust and respect, which could be broken by poor management at any time. Truly advanced lean status should be the final target even for Toyota.

Advanced lean is the organizational status to which we all—not just Toyota—aspire. Ironically, as your organization inches closer to this level of success, the requirements of you as a leader increase tremendously. Your vision and mission are of upmost importance in the early days of your journey, and that importance intensifies with improvement. Without the bold visions of Toyota leaders that spurred the individuals in the organization to solve problems they had not yet known existed, success could have been fleeting. Toyota could have followed the road taken by Studebaker, Nash, and Packard in the United States or Ohta Jidosha and Prince Motor Company in Japan.

You must always revise and present a vision that repositions success for your organization. There is no autopilot. No problem, no kaizen. Cast a vision for your company that makes individuals gasp and proclaim that it is impossible. All the reasons that it is impossible are the problems to be solved that will make it possible. You will continuously welcome problems and find success.

No problem, no kaizen

About the Author

Kiyoshi "Nate" Furuta joined Toyota Motor Corporation in 1970 following his graduation with a law degree from The University of Tokyo. At Toyota, he worked in labor relations and law before being assigned to introduce the company's human resource and management systems outside Japan.

Throughout his 40-year career with Toyota and affiliated companies, spent mostly outside Japan after some early years at the company's headquarters in Toyota City, he spearheaded the development of human resources and general management systems through actual application at strategically critical Toyota organizations in North America and Europe. His development was critical to the company's success in transitioning from a Japanese domestic to a global enterprise. Toyota's management systems have been hailed as exemplary and emulated by countless companies in virtual every industry and on every continent. Nate was instrumental in clarifying the company's tacit knowledge implicit in its philosophy and rationale and translating them into new management practices that were appropriate to each new cultural setting while maintaining the intent and spirit of their original roots in Toyota Japan.

He is retired though may still consult occasionally with executives who wish to seriously study and implement Toyota's management principles and practices. He lives with his wife Sumie in Northern California where they enjoy golfing and gardening, visits with sons Takuya and Hidehisa, and returning for occasional visits to Japan.

Acknowledgements

I could not have published this book without three people: John Shook, Chairman of the Lean Global Network and Senior Advisor of the Lean Enterprise Institute, who as the publisher encouraged me to reorganize this book to be more effective for readers looking for an organization-wide solution to their poor performance; Raquel Arnold, who was my first editor and helped me to organize early drafts; and George Taninecz, whose editing helped to make this book more approachable for readers. Their efforts and encouragement were vital supports for me.

This book is dedicated to my wife Sumie, who has been supporting my life more than 40 years. She enabled me to focus on finding and solving problems in my job, from the labor negotiations during the NUMMI joint venture to turning around massive losses at Toyota Europe.

This book took more than seven years to be published, but I was never discouraged. That is because of my strong and endearing memory of three Toyota executives and teachers: Chairman Fujio Cho; the late Vice Chairman Iwao Isomura; and the late Senior Managing Director Kenzo Tamai, who taught me the precious concepts shown in this book. I knew I had to finish this book to forward their wisdom to the next generation, showing the principles of success through problem finding and problem solving.

Mutual Trust and Mutual Responsibilities at NUMMI

The following are excerpts of the NUMMI contract describing responsibilities of management, the union, and employees:

1-1. The Company's primary objective is to grow and prosper. Since the catalyst for its progress is its employees, it recognizes its obligation to keep them employed and improve their wages and working conditions...

1-2. The Union's primary objective is to improve the quality of life for its members and their families by assuring that they will be treated with dignity and provided with economic security. In addition, it is essential to the Union's purpose to assure the workers are afforded the opportunity to master their work environment; to achieve not only improvement in their economic status but, of equal importance, to gain from their labors a greater measure of dignity, self-fulfillment and self worth. It recognizes, however, the necessity of increasing productivity as a factor in its role in contributing to the development of the Company, which is the source of its member's employment and income.

1-4 Management responsibilities

Company has the exclusive responsibility … to plan, direct, and control Company operations, including items such as products to be manufactured; method of manufacturing or production, and process of manufacturing or assembling; manufacturing, including tools and equipment, schedules, establishment of standardized work; purchase or making of products or services to be incorporated into the products manufactured or processes; establish standards of conduct, including discipline or discharge for good and just cause; hiring, laying off, assigning, transferring, promoting, training and communication with all employees. In performing these responsibilities, the Company will inform the Union about the following matters:

- The inauguration or retirement of top management;
- Annual Company objectives;
- Major organization changes;
- Semi-annual business plans;
- Company's long-range plans and policies;
- Establishment of quarterly production schedules;
- Contemplated insourcing and outsourcing decisions;
- Technological changes that will impact the bargaining unit;
- Other major events.

1-5 Union responsibilities

The Union has the exclusive responsibilities of representing its membership regarding all terms and conditions of employment and to ensure that they are treated consistent with the terms of this Agreement and that they receive fair and equitable wages and benefits. The Union accepts the responsibility to promote the common objectives and to cooperate with the Company in administering, on a fair and equitable basis, standards of conduct; attendance plans and Problem resolution; to promote constant improvement in quality and productivity; and to cooperate with the Company in dealing with governmental entities.

1-6 Employee Responsibilities

The Company and the Union recognize and accept their responsibilities to strive to create and maintain a positive work environment. To accomplish the same for the present and the future, all employees shall have the following responsibilities:

- Support the performance of the total team and actively support other members of the team;

- Meet reasonable team goals and participate in setting of team goals;

- Work within reasonable Company guideline and philosophy;

- Respect the individual rights of others;

- Support and abide by reasonable standard of conduct and attendance policies;

- Promote good housekeeping and maintain a safe work environment;

- Promote kaizen by continually looking for opportunities to make the Company more efficient;

- Achieve quality goals and improve quality standards;

- Support team concept; and

- Assist the Company in meeting production goals and schedules.

Georgetown New-Hire Education Profiles

Education	Team member	Team leader	Group leader
College graduate	14%	35%	57%
Attended college	60%	44%	36%
High school diploma or GED	26%	21%	7%
Total	100%	100%	100%

Georgetown New-Hire Training Courses

Training course	Manager & Assistant manager	Group leader	Team leader	Team member	Specialist	Associate and assistant staff
1. Assimilation	C	C	C	C	C	C
2. Conflict management	C	E			E	
3. Effective meeting facilitation	C	C	C	E**	C	E
4. How to speak so others will listen	E	E			E	E
5. Human resources policy	C	C				
6. Introduction to kaizen*	C	C	C		C	E
7. Intro to problem solving	C	C	C	E**	C	C
8. Job instruction*	E	C	C	E**	E	
9. Job relations	C	C			E	
10. Leader as coach TPS*	E	E	E		E	
11. Leadership	C	C	E**		E	
12. Legal issues	C	C				
13. Listening	E	E	E	E	E	E
14. PDCA applications	C					
15. PDCA introduction	C					
16. Philosophies of efficiency*	C					
17. Practical problem solving	C					
18. Problem solving—level 2	C	C	C		C	E
19. Proposal writing/Docs	C	C			C	C
20. Quality circles facilitation	E	E	E	E	E	E
21. Quality circles participation			E	E		
22. Quality circle promotion	C	C			E	
23. Special office seminars						E
24. Standardized work intro*	C	C	C		C	E
25 Standardized work: office	E				C	E
26. Suggestion sys. training	C	C	E	E	E	E
27. Target selection	E	C	E		E	
28. Worksite communications	E	C	E**		E	E

C = Core course (required)   E = Elective course   E** = part of prepromotion program, does not
*TPS elements   include skilled-trades special training courses

Required Management
Abilities Developed in 1990

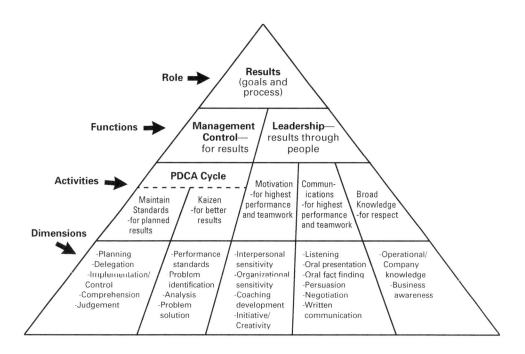

TMEM Hoshin for 2004

Hoshin Statement (Five Year)

Theme 1 — People and Organization

Develop people and organization based on The Toyota Way, to support growing, integrated, and self-reliant European operations.

Theme 2 — Management System

Develop and implement the best management system to consistently lead to high performance.

Theme 3 — Quality and Business Capability

Be capable of providing superior quality products to the customer with shorter lead-time for the majority of European sales.

Theme 4 — Profit and Cost

Increase revenue while reducing cost drastically to build a foundation for sustainable profitability in Europe.

TMEM developed 19 substatements to support the 4 Toyota Europe themes. For example, "Full and effective deployment of Toyota Way as the foundation of working in diverse culture" was one of three statements supporting "People and Organization." The substatement had a measurement defined as "top-rated by Toyota Way assessment outside Japan" and a due date of 2006 (three-year timeframe).

TMEM Annual Hoshin—Substatement Examples

Our THEM annual hoshin contained 28 statements under the four themes of the five-year hoshin statement. As examples of those substatements, below are seven substatements for the People and Organization theme.

Hoshin statement	Target	Timing
1. Deliver Toyota Way training to members across Europe	• Pan-European training-by-grades system in place for executives, focusing problem solving with practical application	03/2005

2. Strengthen safety management in Europe group	• Achieve result to be the safest company in each country (KPI example: lost work cases)
	• Pan-European coordination structure operating:
	  - Pan-Europe safety policy guideline
	  - *Toyota Way in Safety & Health* rolled out
		03/2005
		
		07/2004
		12/2004
		03/2005

3. Establish action plan following motivation survey analysis	• Action plan for top concern in each company: set target following results analysis (KPI example: absentee rate)	12/2004
4. Improve pan-European HR management system for executives	• Development plans in place and development activities started for two successors per position (KPI: successor ratio)	01/2005
5. Improve day-to-day operation by strengthening first-line supervisor capability	• GL Floor Management System pilot course in TMMP • Contents confirmed, ready to deploy in all manufacturing companies	TBD 02/2005
6. Implement effective corporate recruiting strategy	• Start Toyota Europe graduate recruitment	01/2005
7. Develop midterm organizational strategy in Europe	• Total organization plan approved • Consensus with sales and a parent organization	12/2005

Number 2, 3, and 4 were dealt with as day-to-day business and measured by KPIs. In consolidating the European organization, we identified many things as critical goals, partially because a new organization required many things to be established in a short period of time. You should, though, focus on fewer things to have more effective hoshin management.

Hoshin-Assessment Elements for Toyota's Europe Manufacturing Group

In 2003, I was responsible for the Manufacturing hoshin "Accelerate problem identification through visualization to support self-management for better performance in every business unit/function." The 2003 activity was "Each workplace to find, commit to targets, and start tracking performance drivers that support KPI/objective achievements" and targets were "Establish 2003 KPI targets by May 2003, workplace performance drivers in place by November 2003, and meet KPI target by the end of year."

This hoshin, developed based on Total Quality Management (TQM) principles (see *TQM Principles* on page 176), and related activities were very important to the unification of the European Manufacturing companies, and it was important that I improve this aspect of hoshin management.

1. At our half-year review, I evaluated my hoshin achievement as below expectation and in need of improvement. We had established Europe KPI targets, and followed up on these at several meetings, such as Joint Executive Committee or Group Cost Meeting. Furthermore, each company and division had established its own KPIs and performance drivers (e.g., profit and loss and cost reduction charts for Accounting & Finance, ROI of IT investment for Information Systems). But I still could not report the overall picture of integrated KPIs and performance drivers in a single, visual way in order to accelerate problem identification as stated in the hoshin.

2. I reflected on this status, and came to see that I had requested Manufacturing divisions and companies to establish KPIs and drivers and to set up measurements to support Europe-wide KPIs, but I did not communicate how to connect these to each other or who should be responsible for visually coordi-

nating the overall information. To make matters worse, I did not check customers' needs for this information display—each customer had its own style and format. With these reflections in mind, I designated the corporate planning head and his benchmarking staff to visually coordinate the overall information, including providing common definitions. I asked the head of production control and his staff to coordinate customer interests among the manufacturing companies. The result of these efforts was one defined format showing the impact on overall European-wide KPIs.

3. After the data was collected, visually coordinated, and the impact of each KPI and driver shown to division and Manufacturing heads, they became more cooperative in establishing a unified format and visualization method to find problems quicker for overall European performance improvement. They began to understand the direct relation-ship between the performance of their companies to overall results, and they also wanted others to understand their positive contributions to the Manufacturing group.

TQM Principles[1]

Customer-focused	Customer defines quality
Total employee involvement	All employees safely team together and work toward common goals
Process-centered	Steps required to carry out the process aer defined and performance measures continuously monitored to detect unexpected variation
Integrated system	Focus on the horizontal processes interconnecting many different functions and vertically structured departments
Strategic and systematic approach	Strategic planning or strategic management integrates quality as a core component
Continual improvement	Continual improvement to be more competitive and more effective at meeting stakeholder expectations
Fact-based decision making	Continually collect and analyze data in order to improve decision making, foster consensus, and plan based on past performances
Communications	Effective communications of strategies, methods, and timeliness maintains morale and motivates employees throughout the organization

1. Adapted from *The Primary Elements of TQM*, American Society of Quality

ROA Value Tree

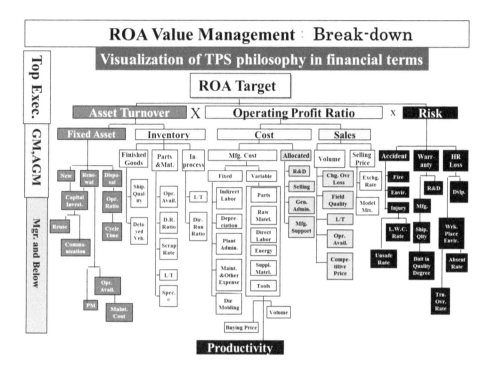

Note: ROA is a financial index, which encourages better use of assets as well as cost or sales control. But you cannot forget fundamentals, including safety, quality, and people. Because of this, safety, quality, and human resources are shown as risks. If these risks are not managed, any gain of ROA could be completely wiped out.

Index